THE COMPACT GUIDE TO

TECH PRODUCT MARKETING

SIMPLIFYING PMM ESSENTIALS FOR ALL LEVELS

EFRAT SHALEM
esmspice.com

TABLE OF CONTENTS

INTRODUCTION

1 Welcome... 6

2 About Me... 8

PRELUDE TO TECH PRODUCT MARKETING

3 What Is Tech Marketing.. 10

4 What Is Tech Product Marketing.. 17

TECH PRODUCT MARKETING IN PRACTICE

5 Tech PMM Responsibilities.. 27

6 Market Research & Competitive Analysis............................. 29

7 Market Segmentation, Customer Profiles & Jobs-To-Be-Done... 36

8 Product Positioning & Messaging....................................... 45

9 Go-To-Market Strategy... 53

10 Sales & Customer Success Enablement............................... 60

SOLUTIONS TO COMMON DISPUTES

11 Pricing.. 67

12 Content Development.. 79

13 Product Feature Suggestions......................... 83

14 Product User Journey Optimization.............. 85

15 Product Communication.................................. 88

TECH PRODUCT MARKETING MANAGERS

16 B2B & B2C Tech Product Marketing............... 91

17 Tech PMM Hiring Process & Career Advancement.......................... 94

FINAL WORDS

18 Tech Product Marketing Summary................. 101

INTRODUCTION

WELCOME

Welcome to *The Compact Guide To Tech Product Marketing*!

Throughout this book, you will gain insights from my professional experiences, learn the secrets of the trade, and equip yourself with tools that have proven to be game-changers in the world of tech product marketing!

Whether you are a budding tech product marketer, a tech product marketing manager seeking to enhance your workflow, a professional wishing to introduce the PMM role to a high-tech team, an entrepreneur looking to promote your venture, or a tech business leader contemplating a hire - this guide is designed for you!

Embark on a profound exploration as we unravel the true essence of product marketing in the high-tech industry. We will delve into practical applications, offering a detailed panorama of tech PMM responsibilities —from market research to sales enablement; Provide pragmatic solutions to common challenges like pricing and content development; Define the distinctive roles of B2C and B2B tech product marketing managers, highlighting the essential traits they embody; And conclude with vital insights to guide you on your exciting tech product marketing path!

UNMATCHED BOOK ADVANTAGES

- The most comprehensive yet compact tech product marketing-focused guide.
- Authored by a professional with over a decade of experience in marketing, product management, and entrepreneurship in the high-tech sector.
- Packed with real-world examples and insights from both the B2B and B2C tech industries.
- Includes meticulously crafted tech PMM templates and infographics.

This book will be your PMM guide, mentor, and companion. Let's innovate, inspire, and make a lasting impact!

ABOUT ME

My name is Efrat Shalem, and for the past decade, I have been deeply immersed in the high-tech landscape. As a specialist in marketing and product management, as well as an impact entrepreneur, I have been at the forefront of establishing startups and guiding them towards leaving a significant imprint on global markets.

I gained vast experience in transforming ideas into products and brands, leading strategy, go-to-market, and growth for B2B and B2C companies in various verticals including AI, big data, IoT, smart mobility, cloud, eCommerce, and fintech. I crafted marketing strategies that landed big customers like IBM, Snap Inc., Turner, and Mercedes-Benz and helped attain millions of dollars in investments.

I hold a double BA in Communication and Middle Eastern and African History from Tel Aviv University, and what truly fuels my drive is my unwavering passion for technology and its transformative power to better lives.

Join me on a journey to uncover the core principles of product marketing, the strategies underpinning success, and the essential skills required to expertly manage and promote cutting-edge tech products.

Sincerely yours,

Efrat Shalem

PRELUDE TO TECH PRODUCT MARKETING

WHAT IS TECH MARKETING

Before we delve into the depths of product marketing, let's ensure we understand what marketing is and why it's so important for tech companies to nurture their marketing efforts.

For this purpose, I love to start with Apple's famous "Think Different" campaign launch event from back in 1997, presented by no other than the late founder and CEO, Steve Jobs.

I urge you to watch this inspiring display of marketing extravaganza on my YouTube channel. Once you finish watching, we will analyze the thorough strategic thinking behind Jobs's brilliant marketing speech.

> **"We have to be really clear on what we want them to know about us."**
>
> **– Steve Jobs, Founder & CEO, Apple Inc.**

Feeling inspired? Awesome! Now let's get down to marketing.

"THINK DIFFERENT" SPEECH - KEY TAKEAWAYS

- According to Jobs, "marketing is about values", and so the "Think Different" mantra is all about the unique value proposition. It's about not just doing what everyone else does, but rather innovating, standing out, and positioning our products or services differently to provide unique value to our customers. Jobs also adds that the core values of the company shouldn't change as the company grows, they're its DNA, what sets it apart from competitors, and it is marketing's job to make those core values known and maintained throughout the customer experience with the brand, product, and services.

- Then, Jobs talks about celebrating the customer. A company should remember that its only justification for existence is the value it brings its customers. Therefore, its marketing messages should reflect and honor the customers' personalities, needs, and dreams – not its product features. At the 1997 Worldwide Developer Conference, which you can also view on my YouTube channel, Jobs even said that to achieve product-market fit we should always start with the customer experience and work backward to the technology, since a problem or need must be identified before creating a solution.

> "You've got to start with the customer experience and work backward to the technology. You can't start with the technology and then try to figure out where to sell it."
>
> – Steve Jobs, Founder & CEO, Apple Inc.

- Jobs also reminds and emphasizes what Appel is all about, its beliefs, and core values because he understood that customers want to know who is behind the company, what they believe in, and what they stand for as a collective. Business is all about people, and people need to trust your business to do business with you. It's marketing's job to make sure you are crafting the right messages to the right people at the right time, so you can get the customers, keep them satisfied and coming back.

- In addition, Jobs clarifies that every brand, regardless of how well-known it is, needs investment both financially and creatively, and even though most people might take Apple's commercial success for granted, he openly admits that Apple invested millions of dollars in brand advertising campaigns. He makes sure the audience understands that there's no magical trick to earn this magnitude of success, just creative thinking, continuous innovation, hard work, and yes, a lot of money.

TECH MARKETING BUDGET

If we look at how much it costs to build an effective revenue-generating tech marketing department today, we'll find that similar to Apple in 1997, technology companies are allocating a significant portion of their budget to marketing. In fact, they rank third in marketing expenditures, devoting 15% of their total budget to it, and are surpassed only by the consumer packaged goods and services industries.

Their budget is divided into expenses for hiring a marketing team, training their employees, doing research and analysis, executing campaigns, and ongoing operations.

Figure 1: Marketing Budgets By Industry

Marketing accounts for what percentage of your overall budget?

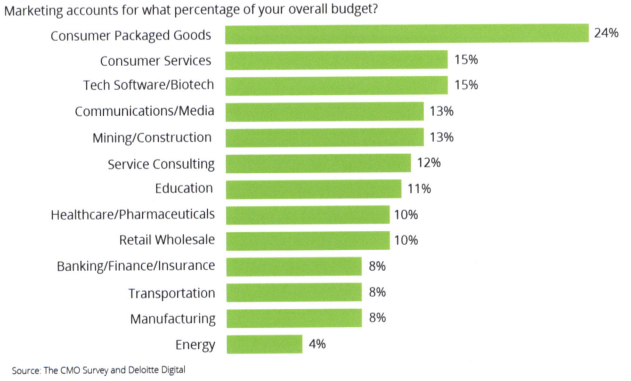

Source: The CMO Survey and Deloitte Digital

Figure 2: Marketing Expenses by Industry

Marketing expenses in your company include the following (check all that apply):

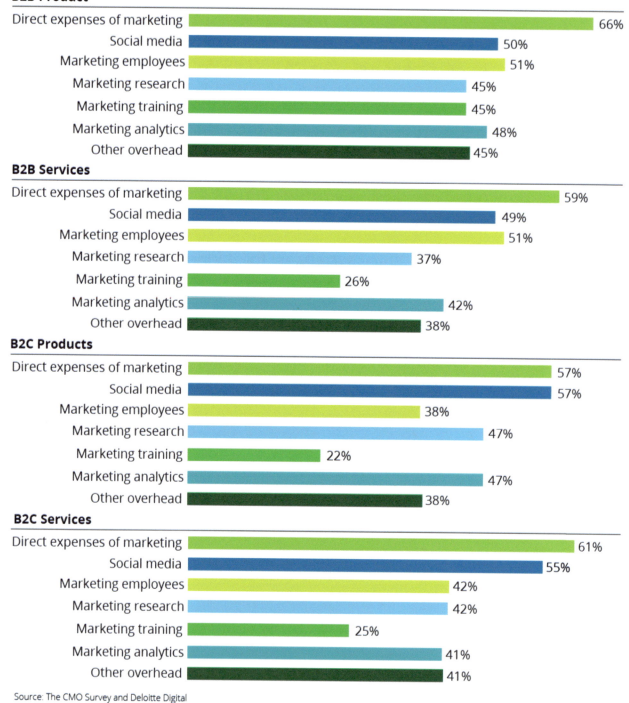

B2B Product

Direct expenses of marketing	66%
Social media	50%
Marketing employees	51%
Marketing research	45%
Marketing training	45%
Marketing analytics	48%
Other overhead	45%

B2B Services

Direct expenses of marketing	59%
Social media	49%
Marketing employees	51%
Marketing research	37%
Marketing training	26%
Marketing analytics	42%
Other overhead	38%

B2C Products

Direct expenses of marketing	57%
Social media	57%
Marketing employees	38%
Marketing research	47%
Marketing training	22%
Marketing analytics	47%
Other overhead	38%

B2C Services

Direct expenses of marketing	61%
Social media	55%
Marketing employees	42%
Marketing research	42%
Marketing training	25%
Marketing analytics	41%
Other overhead	41%

Source: The CMO Survey and Deloitte Digital

THE TECH MARKETING DEPARTMENT

Tech marketing departments are usually led by a chief marketing officer (CMO) or a VP of marketing and are composed of these five teams:

- **Growth –** owns the company's digital assets and is generally responsible for their operation, user cycle tracking, and optimization [There are companies where the Marketing Growth team is united with the Product Growth team and together they constitute an independent growth department].

- **Content –** writes and edits the company's blog, case studies, webinars, video scripts, and podcasts.

- **Communication –** manages the company's brand awareness, social media, newsletters, PR, and conferences.

- **Design –** crafts the branding and online and offline marketing materials.

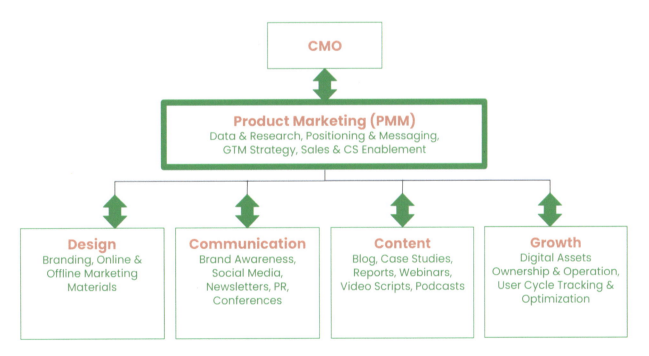

Marketing Department Structure

CMO

Product Marketing (PMM)
Data & Research, Positioning & Messaging, GTM Strategy, Sales & CS Enablement

Design
Branding, Online & Offline Marketing Materials

Communication
Brand Awareness, Social Media, Newsletters, PR, Conferences

Content
Blog, Case Studies, Reports, Webinars, Video Scripts, Podcasts

Growth
Digital Assets Ownership & Operation, User Cycle Tracking & Optimization

- And, of course, **Product Marketing -** sets the marketing foundations for the entire company by researching and analyzing market and product data, doing positioning and messaging, planning go-to-market strategies, and managing the sales and customer success enablement kits.

To summarize, marketing plays a pivotal role in the tech industry.
It entails the process of identifying, anticipating, and satisfying customer needs effectively and profitably. It involves strategies and tactics to communicate, promote, and sell products or services.

Now that we understand the importance of marketing in high-tech, let's delve into the realm of product marketing. We'll explore its intricacies and discover how to become, as well as recruit, top-notch tech product marketing managers.

WHAT IS TECH PRODUCT MARKETING

Now it's time to figure out the essence of tech product marketing. To do this, I consulted ChatGPT, the renowned AI model trained on extensive web datasets, to capture the most precise and widely accepted definition of tech product marketing. Thus, according to ChatGPT:

"Product marketing is the key connector between technical product development and commercial gain, leveraging its understanding of the technology, market dynamics, and customer needs to drive product success."

Product marketing is where the product and customer meet. It focuses on understanding market and customer needs, influencing product development, defining go-to-market strategies, and promoting products to customers and prospects. Product marketing is about delivering the right product to the right customer at the right time. It involves positioning the product in a way that resonates with the target audience, creating effective messaging, launching marketing plans, and supporting sales and customer success.

But, where does this vital function best fit within a company? Is it in the product or the marketing department? The tech industry doesn't seem to have a straightforward answer.

Therefore, I went ahead and asked a group of professional product marketing and product managers in which department product marketing management sits in their company, plus, which department is the right department for this function, in their opinion:

Tech PMM Placement Survey 2023

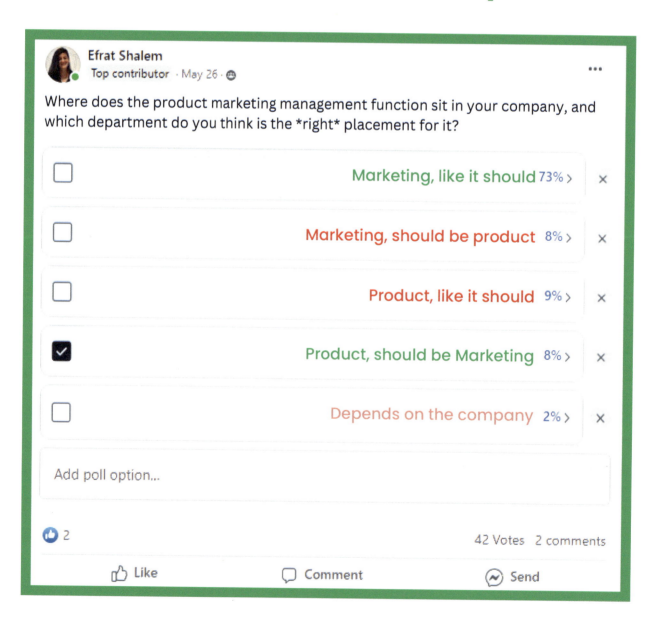

Out of 42 PMM and PM professionals surveyed, a significant 73% stated that their PMM is rightly positioned within the Marketing Department, and an additional 8% mentioned their PMM is currently in the Product Department but believed it should be in Marketing. Yet, 17% of respondents felt that the Product Department is the appropriate place for a PMM.

The confusion often stems from the name "Product Marketing". However, if you follow the previous chapters, it is clear that product marketing is primarily a marketing role. In essence, it lays the groundwork for all marketing messages and initiatives.

Think of the product marketing manager as the marketing strategist, mirroring the product manager who serves as the product strategist. Both roles are pivotal in defining the company's value proposition and setting the foundational pillars for its overall operations.

Thus, I not only advocate placing product marketing managers within the marketing department but firmly believe that the initial marketing role to be filled in a company should be that of a product marketer.

This strategic move ensures that the foundation of the company's marketing game plan is expertly established before spending money on marketing campaigns so they would have the right messages targeted to the right audience at the right time and on the most appropriate platforms.

Simultaneously, they should maintain a strong collaboration with the product department and others to craft a cohesive strategy that resonates with both the company's values and the customer's needs.

Product Workflow

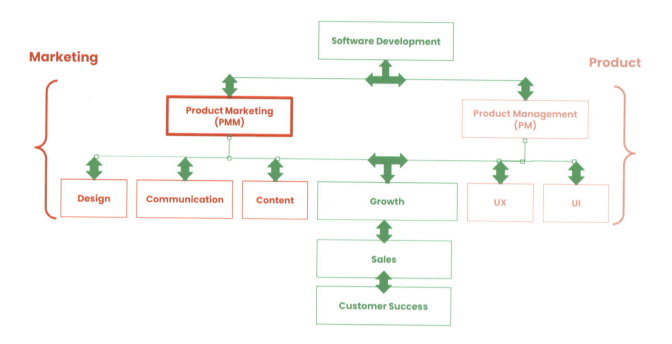

Now, let's explore the product workflow among the various departments in a standard tech company. Naturally, there's the software development department which practically builds the company's products, defining its stature as a high-tech entity.

The software development department operates based on the direction and key performance indicators (KPIs) established by the product management team. The PM team, housed within the product department, also steers the user interface (UI) and user experience (UX) design teams to craft a product tailored to customer needs.

Next, the marketing department is steered by the product marketing team. They collaborate closely with the product management team, ensuring new products align with appropriate messaging. They also ensure these products target the right market via the most effective platforms, establishing core marketing principles. The marketing design, communication, and content teams then build on these principles for their initiatives.

The growth department, positioned at the crossroads of the product and marketing teams, manages and monitors operations concerning acquisition, retention, renewal, and cancellation in the customer journey.

The sales department then steps in, converting marketing-generated leads into actual customers. Lastly, the customer success department continually supports and delights customers, ensuring their ongoing satisfaction and product usage, all in the interest of sustaining the business.

It is important to note that the workflow is not unidirectional. Each department or team can gather insights from the market, competitors, or customer behavior that may shape the strategy of another department or team. Therefore, preventing working in silos through data sharing and open communication channels is essential to ensure cohesive collaboration and a harmonious experience throughout the customer journey.

PMM Internal Stakeholders

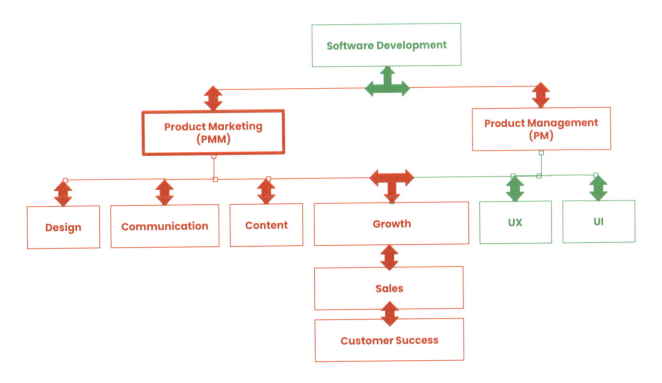

With that being said, the PMM will primarily liaise with the product management, marketing design, communication, content, growth, sales, and customer success teams. This collaboration ensures alignment between the product's values and the customer's expectations and needs.

Besides internal stakeholders, the value creation in product marketing stems from:

- Delving into the company's product features and analyzing customer usability metrics.

- Investigating the market, encompassing competitive analysis, industry segmentation (for B2B), end-user segmentation (for B2C), and multi-channel marketing analytics.

- Identifying sales stakeholders, personas, and Jobs-To-Be-Done, and gathering feedback from existing customers.

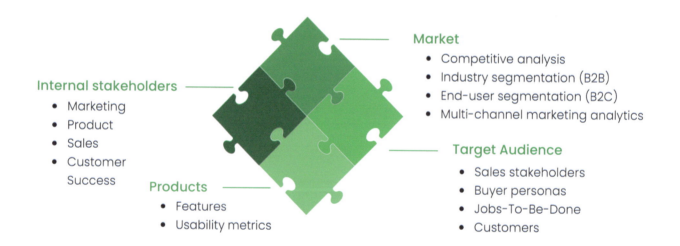

COMMON BUSINESS MODELS

In the high-tech industry, there are three common types of business models: business-to-consumer (B2C), business-to-business (B2B), and business-to-government (B2G), and a company chooses its marketing strategy by the type of buyers that it is trying to acquire.

For example, Apple uses a B2C business model when it offers tech products designed primarily for end-users, such as iPhones, iPads, and Macs, by selling them directly to consumers.

On the other hand, IBM uses the B2B business model by offering cloud computing, artificial intelligence, data analytics, and various software and hardware solutions to other businesses.

In addition, Lockheed Martin, a global leader in aerospace defense-related products, uses a B2G business model to sell its technology to various government entities.

There's also a business-to-business-to-consumer (B2B2C) business model where two companies provide complementary goods or services to reach the same end consumer.

For example, Google uses a B2B2C business model on its search engine because it sells advertising solutions to businesses that target consumers who browse the web, effectively connecting companies directly with end-users.

A company can adopt a single business model or blend multiple models based on its products and market demand, and product marketers should adjust their marketing strategy accordingly.

B2C	B2B	B2G	B2B2C
Business-to-Consumer	Business-to-Business	Business-to-Government	Business-to-Business-to-Consumer
Apple	IBM	Lockheed Martin	Google
Sells iPhones, iPads, and Macs directly to consumers	Sells cloud computing, artificial intelligence, data analytics, and various software and hardware solutions to other businesses	Sells aerospace and defense-related products to various government entities	Sells advertising solutions to businesses that are targeting consumers browsing its search engine

BUSINESS MODEL CANVAS

A favored tool among entrepreneurs is the Business Model Canvas, a strategic management template from the best-selling management book *Business Model Generation*. It aids in positioning startups within the market and crystallizing their unique value proposition (UVP). Used globally by leading organizations and startups, it allows teams to describe, design, innovate, and adapt their business models.

Problem	Solution	Unique Value Proposition	Unfair Advantages	Market Segments
What is the problem that you are solving for your customers? The lack of integration between Google products is causing PMs to waste time on manually synchronizing all of the data they've input in multiple notes and sheets.	**How do you solve your customers' problem?** A complete integrated and automated PM Suite leveraging our existing products.	**What is your unique selling point?** PM Suite integrates the PM's most-used product data tools and automates the entire PM process including ideation, backlog prioritization, task managing, calendar meetings, and PM templates to improve organization, team collaboration, and time management while saving money for startup PMs.	**What elements make your solution better than your competitors?** • Integration between our products • Automation of our products • Many PMs are already using our products • Free software included in our products	**How do you differentiate your customers?** • Corporates • Startups • Agencies • Freelancers
	Key Metrics		**Channels**	**Personas**
	How do you measure success? 1. PM Suite data size 2. No. of PM users 3. % of automated inputs confirmed by users		**How do your personas hear about your business?** • ProductHunt • Quora • LinkedIn • Facebook • Medium • Online courses • Hackathons	**What are the key customer archetypes that you are serving?** • Old-School PMs • Remote PMs • No-Budget Modern PMs

Cost Structure	Revenue Streams	Competitors
What are the important costs you pay to deliver the value proposition? Product-led: Expenses mainly on software development, marketing, and customer support.	**How do you make money?** Monthly payment / Freemium / Pay per export / Drive data size	**Who are you competing with in the industry?** 1. ProductBoard 2. ProdPad 3. ProjectManager

When joining a new tech company as a PMM, this tool can prove invaluable. It offers a concise overview of the business model, UVP, primary competitors, target markets, personas, and the existing marketing strategy.

I strongly advise reaching out to your company's business leaders or founders to obtain this document or collaborate with them in creating a new one. This will ensure a solid understanding of the business fundamentals, allowing you to start generating product marketing value quickly.

To summarize, tech product marketing is a marketing function that seamlessly integrates customer insights with product development, guiding go-to-market strategies, positioning, and support for sales and customer success teams.

Next, we'll dive into the practical facets of tech product marketing, unveiling best practices and effective strategies.

TECH PRODUCT MARKETING IN PRACTICE

TECH PMM RESPONSIBILITIES

Many high-tech companies are recruiting product marketing managers, but each company defines the position differently. That's why I created an online survey in the largest Facebook group for PMMs in Israel and asked them to mark all the areas of responsibility that sit under them directly as part of their role in their high-tech company (that is, areas in which they are trusted daily and not just helping others when needed) so that we get the most accurate reflection of the PMM position in the high-tech market today.

Tech PMM Responsibilities Survey 2023

The 418 responses highlighted the varied nature of the PMM role, with the highest voted responsibility, **Product Positioning & Messaging**, receiving only 13% of the votes.

The other most frequently cited PMM duties include:

- **Market Research & Competitive Analysis**
- **Market Segmentation, Customer Profiles & Jobs-To-Be-Done**
- **High-Level Go-To-Market (GTM) Strategy**
- **Sales & Customer Success Enablement**

We'll delve into understanding each of these areas in detail.

Moreover, there are several responsibilities often associated with PMMs that spark debate, such as:

- **Pricing**
- **Content Development**
- **Product Feature Suggestions**
- **Product User Journey Optimization**
- **Product Communication**

We'll explore each of these responsibilities to determine who should ideally own them in a high-tech company.

MARKET RESEARCH & COMPETITIVE ANALYSIS

MARKET RESEARCH

Market research involves gathering, analyzing, and interpreting information about a specific market. For tech start-ups and well-established tech companies, continuous market research is essential due to the rapidly evolving nature of the industry. To secure a substantial market share, it's crucial for tech companies to not only conduct regular research but also to implement the insights derived promptly before consumer trends change again.

As product marketing stands at the crossroads of product development and the market, acting as the voice of the customer within the company, it has a pivotal role in shaping the company's go-to-market strategy through effective market research. The end goal of conducting market research is to help you make informed decisions about how to scale your company.

Market Share

Key reasons for undertaking market research encompass:

- Gaining deep insights into the target market
- Recognizing competitors within your niche
- Identifying and growing in emerging subsectors
- Evaluating the viability of a new business concept
- Understanding how new marketing trends apply to your venture
- Measuring the demand for current or prospective products/features
- Enhancing efforts by deeply understanding customer preferences

The process of planning and conducting the research alone can often give you a deeper understanding of your company, product, and vision for growth.

Market Metrics

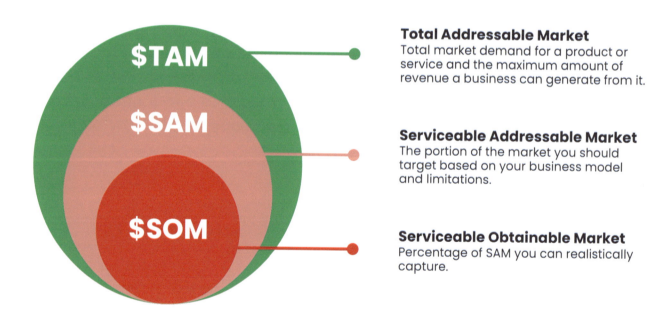

Total Addressable Market
Total market demand for a product or service and the maximum amount of revenue a business can generate from it.

Serviceable Addressable Market
The portion of the market you should target based on your business model and limitations.

Serviceable Obtainable Market
Percentage of SAM you can realistically capture.

When launching a new startup or product, it's important to calculate your industry's market share. TAM, SAM, and SOM are acronyms for three metrics to describe the market your organization operates in - Total Addressable Market, Serviceable Addressable Market, and Serviceable Obtainable Market. These metrics are key components of a business plan, particularly as you craft your product marketing strategy and choose to enter the markets that are worth your time and resources.

You can find these and other metrics using two methods:

1. **Primary research** - gathered by the company, usually by the marketing and product teams or by an outside firm it hires. Primary information is the unique data that you collect yourself. While more time-consuming, you have complete control over how your data is sourced and analyzed.

2. **Secondary research** - draws on external sources of data. Secondary information is data that has been previously collected and is available for review online or offline. The data may be published in white papers, market reports, trade journals, newspapers, or websites. Secondary information is relatively easy to collect; however, you cannot control how the data was collected or interpreted. Furthermore, the information you find will also be easily accessible to your competitors.

Primary Research

- Surveys
- Interviews
- Focus groups
- Observational studies
- User testing

Secondary Research

- Published market research reports
  - Gartner
  - Frost & Sullivan
  - Forrester
  - Marketresearch.com
  - IDC
- Consumer and industry trends sites
  - Statista
  - CompTIA.org
  - TechCrunch
- Government statistics sites
  - The US Government's Business Dynamics Statistics
  - European Data Portal
- Company insights sites
  - Crunchbase
  - Israel's Startup Nation Finder
  - Product Hunt
- SEO and competitor research sites
  - SEMRush
  - SimilarWeb
- Competitors' websites and social networks

In addition, competitors' websites and social networks are often a valuable starting point for your market research. Both public and private companies typically reveal a lot of information about their services or product offerings that can be leveraged for your strategic decisions based on the market research they already did. Publicly traded companies also publish annual reports and other presentations for their investors, which can demonstrate how an established company is faring in your targeted sector.

COMPETITIVE ANALYSIS

In the dynamic realm of technology, the sands of competition shift quickly. Being ahead isn't just about innovating; it's about understanding what's happening around you.

"Competitive analysis is essentially your secret weapon in understanding your market position relative to others. It's a systematic process where you evaluate your competitor's strategies to determine their strengths and weaknesses relative to your product or service."

As a PMM, you are positioned at the intersection of the product and its market. You understand the product features and benefits and are acutely aware of the market needs and desires. When you lead the competitive analysis, you're not just gathering data; you're gaining insights to shape product development, inform marketing strategies, and ensure that your company's offering resonates deeply with its audience.

Here's why competitive analysis is critical for tech companies:

- **The pace of innovation:** In the tech world, innovations emerge at a breakneck speed. Today's unique feature could be tomorrow's industry standard.

- **Market differentiation:** By understanding what everyone else is doing, you can find gaps in the market or potential areas where your product can stand out and define your unique value proposition.

- **Anticipation:** By understanding your competitors, you can sometimes predict their next moves and strategize accordingly.

Now, here's how to conduct a competitive analysis:

- **Identify key competitors:** Know who you are up against. Look at market leaders, emerging players, and even potential entrants.

- **Analyze product offerings:** Dive deep into their products. What features do they promote? What pricing strategies do they use?

- **Study marketing and sales tactics:** How do they position themselves? What channels do they use? How do they engage with their audience?

- **Gather customer feedback:** Look at reviews, forums, and feedback. What do customers love or hate about the competition?

In conclusion, mastering competitive analysis isn't just a skill; it's a necessity. In your journey as a PMM, it will be an invaluable tool in your arsenal, helping you steer your company to success in the competitive Red Ocean and the new sparsely populated Blue Ocean. Dive deep, stay curious, and always be ready to adapt.

THE NEED	ALTERNATIVE FIX
What are the Jobs-To-Be-Done that the customers are looking to do or achieve	What alternative tools and methods the customers are currently using to handle this challenge

BENEFITS	THE PAIN
What key benefits customers are gaining by using these alternative fixes	What is not working in the way customers are currently handling this challenge

LIMITATIONS	EFFECT
What customers are compromising by implementing their current fix	What is the negative effect these limitations have on the customers' business/work/life

COST	DISCOVERY
How much customers are currently paying for alternative fixes to get the job done	How customers learn about these alternatives

OUR SOLUTION	KEY FEATURES
What is the unique solution we are offering to tackle this need/pain	What are the key product features our solution offers to help solve this need/pain

UNFAIR ADVANTAGES	GAPS
What are the unique advantages our solution offers that set it apart from other alternatives	What our solution still lacks and plans to bridge

USE CASES	IMPACT
What are the ideal use cases that our solution fits	What is the positive impact our solution has on the customers' business/work/life

VALUE FOR MONEY	REVELATION
How much customers are paying us to get the job done	How customers learn about our solution

MARKET SEGMENTATION, CUSTOMER PROFILES & JOBS-TO-BE-DONE

MARKET SEGMENTATION

Market segmentation is an extension of market research that seeks to identify targeted groups of customers to tailor products and brands in a way that is appealing to them.

By segmenting the market effectively, companies can mitigate risk, identify the most promising products for target markets, and determine the best way to deliver the products to them. This allows companies to optimize resource allocation for the best return on investment, also known as ROI.

Therefore, once your business model is established, whether targeting consumers, businesses, or governments, it's crucial to segment them into categories.

Primary Types of Market Segmentation

DEMOGRAPHIC

Segmentation by age, income, gender, race, education, or occupation.

FIRMOGRAPHIC

Segmentation by industry, company size, customer base, number of offices, or annual revenue.

GEOGRAPHIC

Segmentation based on the customers' physical location.

BEHAVIORAL

Segmentation based on the customers' past interactions with products or markets.

PSYCHOGRAPHIC

Segmentation based on the customers' lifestyle, personality, opinions, or interests.

There are five primary types of market segmentation:

- **Demographic** - a common approach that categorizes the market based on characteristics like age, income, gender, race, education, or occupation. This strategy operates on the premise that individuals with comparable demographics share similar needs.

- **Firmographic** - parallels demographic segmentation but focuses on organizations rather than individuals. This approach examines attributes like industry, company size, customer base, number of offices, or annual revenue.

- **Geographic** - often considered a subset of demographic segmentation. It clusters customers based on their physical location, underlining the notion that individuals in a specific area might have shared needs. This tactic is particularly beneficial for larger companies looking to branch out into diverse regions or locations.

- **Behavioral** - centers on analyzing consumer actions and decision-making trends. It categorizes consumers based on their past interactions with products or markets, positing that past spending behaviors can forecast future purchasing tendencies. However, it's essential to note that spending patterns can evolve over time or due to significant global occurrences.

- **Psychographic** - a challenging yet powerful method, that categorizes consumers based on their lifestyle, personality, opinions, or interests. While this approach can be tricky due to the fluid nature of these traits and the potential lack of concrete data, it often offers robust results by grouping individuals based on their intrinsic motivations rather than mere external factors.

In B2B models, it's often wise to segment the target market using firmographic segmentation, starting by identifying the most suitable and potentially profitable industries for their products.

Certain industries tend to invest more in technological advancements. According to Statista, leading the tech adoption curve currently are sectors like software, tech hosting, financial services, retail, and e-commerce. While transportation, healthcare, consumer goods, and industrial products follow closely, showing considerable IT expenditure and openness to emerging technologies.

Firmographic Segmentation

Industries differ not only in their investment in technology but also in their willingness to be early adopters. If your product is at the cutting edge, aim for sectors that are more inclined to experiment with innovations. For instance, if you offer business process automation (BPA) software, banks, logistics firms, and industrial enterprises could be your prime audience. A marketing tool might resonate more with retailers and service providers, while a video conferencing solution could be apt for educational institutions, medical organizations, and global enterprises.

Moreover, the potential market size within each industry is crucial. Some sectors inherently offer broader scopes for growth due to their vastness. So, when strategizing, it's essential to weigh the industry's technological receptivity against its sheer size and adaptability.

One of the best ways to identify the ideal industry for your product is to analyze the sectors where your competitors are currently operating. Assess whether there is an opportunity for your company within that industry, whether your competitors have already saturated it, and what strategies you can deploy to compete effectively. After determining your primary industries, pivot your attention to your company's key internal stakeholders to ensure alignment.

CUSTOMER PROFILES

Once you identified your go-to industries, you should plan to develop buyer personas for each of your sector segments. A buyer persona is a detailed representation of your ideal customer based on deep research of your existing or desired audience.

They usually encompass not only demographic information like age, location, and income but also psychographic information like interests, motivations, and concerns in their purchasing decision. These personas will help guide the development of your product and plan your marketing efforts. For example, rather than sending generic lead nurturing emails to your entire database, segmenting by buyer persona lets you customize your messages based on the unique attributes of each persona.

There isn't a set list of universally recognized buyer personas to choose from, this is why I recommend using buyer persona templates and generators, which you can find online. Also, it is important to collaborate with other departments in your company like sales, customer success, and product, as each department has unique experiences with the customers that will serve as valuable information in identifying your buyer personas.

It's also critical to distinguish between B2C and B2B buyer personas. For the business-to-consumer model, prospective customers are individuals or families, and their decision to buy your products or services depends on their buying power. Based on their needs, they might not need a long time to consider if they want your products or services. Marketing B2C products or services can also be done through a broad customer base.

On the other hand, marketing business-to-business products or services needs to be handled differently. This is because the ideal customer is composed of multiple personas in different roles. There are varying interests, concerns, and goals, so the customer journey can take a while. In addition, the decision-makers may not be the end-users of the product or service.

B2B Buyer Persona

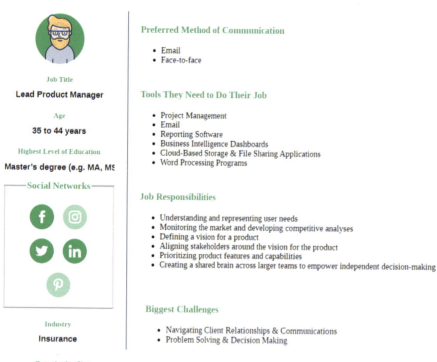

Job Title

Lead Product Manager

Age

35 to 44 years

Highest Level of Education

Master's degree (e.g. MA, MS

Social Networks

Industry

Insurance

Organization Size

201-500 employees

Preferred Method of Communication

- Email
- Face-to-face

Tools They Need to Do Their Job

- Project Management
- Email
- Reporting Software
- Business Intelligence Dashboards
- Cloud-Based Storage & File Sharing Applications
- Word Processing Programs

Job Responsibilities

- Understanding and representing user needs
- Monitoring the market and developing competitive analyses
- Defining a vision for a product
- Aligning stakeholders around the vision for the product
- Prioritizing product features and capabilities
- Creating a shared brain across larger teams to empower independent decision-making

Biggest Challenges

- Navigating Client Relationships & Communications
- Problem Solving & Decision Making

Their Job Is Measured By

- No. of Active Users
- No. of Paying Customers
- Retention Percentage
- Revenue

Reports to

- CEO
- CTO
- VP Product

Goals or Objectives

- Active Users
- Paying Users
- Returning Users
- Conversion Rates
- Revenue

They Gain Information By

- Online Courses
- Conferences
- Blogs & Vlogs
- Case Studies
- Competitor Research

Make My Persona by HubSpot

That's why for B2B models you need to turn your attention inward and recognize the prevalent sales stakeholders within each target industry. Understanding your sales stakeholders' type allows you to tailor the company's go-to-market techniques for a more targeted approach.

There are six main sales stakeholder types:

Sales Stakeholders

End User

Interacts with the product and evaluates its post-purchase performance

Recommender

Has specific expertise about the product and analyzes its pros & cons

Buyer

Analyzes the financial part of the sale, compares it to other offerings, negotiates and approves the price & terms

Gatekeeper

Controls information and communication for the buyer's team, and often is the first and ongoing point of contact

Influencer

Respected and consulted for their opinions. Has a real impact on the perception and choices of the decision makers

Decision Maker

Often a senior-level executive, gives the final approval or denial of the sale

Illustrations by Storyset

Since it's a generalization, keep in mind that a real-life customer can have characteristics of several types. Catering to sales stakeholders' specific needs and preferences can help you optimize their interactions with your company, enhance their buying experience, and ultimately boost sales.

A user story is an informal, general explanation of a software product or feature written from the perspective of the end user. Its purpose is to articulate how a product or feature will provide value to the customer. User stories are often expressed in a simple sentence, structured as follows:

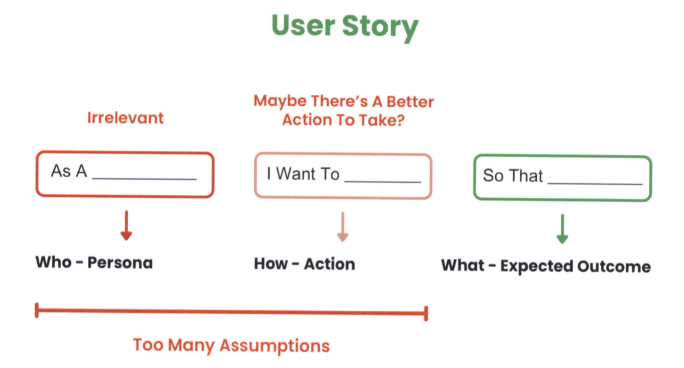

Example:

As a <u>sales manager called Joe</u>, I want to <u>understand my colleagues' progress quickly and thoroughly</u>, so that <u>I can better report our successes and failures to my superiors</u>.

That said, personas work well when the user base can be broken down into different types of users with different needs, but when building a product, that's not always the case.

JOBS-TO-BE-DONE

For some products, especially ones that use business-to-consumer models, customers come in all shapes and sizes, from all countries, all backgrounds, all salaries, and all levels of computer skills. The only thing in common is the job they need to get done. In these cases, it's best to get an intimate understanding of the job itself, what creates demand for it, and why.

This framework, called Jobs-To-Be-Done (JTBD), emerged in the early 1990s as a helpful way to look at customer motivations rather than customer attributes. It aims to help you understand the real jobs customers use your product for.

> "...People don't want a quarter-inch drill, they want a quarter-inch hole."
>
> **- Theodore Levitt, Economist and Harvard Business School Professor**

This theory is based on the notion that products match problems, not people, and that the outcome a person wants is much more important than the person themselves.

In this method, we'll use job stories, a different way of designing and promoting products and features, and they are structured as follows:

Job Story

When _____	I Want To _____	So That _____
↓	↓	↓
When – Situation	**Why – Motivation**	**What – Expected Outcome**

Example:
When <u>I need to report my team's successes and failures to my superiors,</u> I want to <u>explain well why they occurred,</u> so that <u>I can gain my superiors' trust and respect</u>.

So the actual job the customers hire your product to do is gaining the trust and respect of their work superiors.

By focusing on the job and the context of the customers, you can develop and market well-tailored products and messages that will match what customers are already trying to achieve when they are trying to achieve it.

PRODUCT POSITIONING & MESSAGING

POSITIONING

Tech product positioning defines how a company will market and sell its software or hardware product. A well-thought-out strategy can set a product apart from its competitors and underscore its key advantages for customers.

> "Product positioning is the process of determining new products' position in the minds of consumers. It includes analyzing the market and competitors' positions, defining the position of a new product among the existing ones, and communicating a particular brand's product image."
>
> – SendPulse

Therefore, harnessing empathy and paying attention to what your customers think is crucial to anticipate their reception of the product post-launch.

POSITIONING STRATEGIES

Let's explore the five key product positioning strategies that will help you define the position of your product:

1. Characteristics-based positioning - In this strategy, brands assign specific characteristics to their products to foster associations, guiding consumers to choose based on brand image and product attributes. Consider the world of antivirus software, for instance. A user primarily concerned about multi-device protection might lean towards McAfee because of its positioning on comprehensive coverage. Conversely, a user who values lightweight and speedy software might gravitate towards Bitdefender.

2. Use or application-based positioning - In this strategy, companies position themselves by associating with a certain use or application. For instance, Adobe Photoshop is often associated with professional graphic design and photo editing, making it the go-to for designers and photographers. On the other hand, tools like Canva have positioned themselves for easy and quick design solutions, appealing to businesses and individuals who want to create attractive designs without the steep learning curve of professional software.

3. Competitor-based positioning - This strategy emphasizes a brand's unique strengths in comparison to rivals in the same sector. Competitor-based positioning can be keenly observed in the long-standing rivalry between Apple's Mac and Microsoft's PC. Both have taken direct jabs at each other in advertising campaigns to highlight their respective strengths. Apple's "Get a Mac" commercials personified the two platforms, portraying Mac as the young, hip counterpart to the stodgier PC. Microsoft, in response, launched campaigns emphasizing the vast versatility and affordability of PCs. Through these campaigns, each brand leveraged its competitor's image to accentuate its own unique selling propositions.

4. Quality or prestige-based positioning - The brands that are using this strategy don't concentrate on their price point; they focus on their prestige or high quality instead. Sometimes, it's the reputation that makes a brand attract customers. Let's take Apple, for example. Its sleek and innovative designs have built a reputation for high-quality, premium products that cater to a certain lifestyle and image. Their emphasis on design, user experience, and a dedicated ecosystem has attracted customers who appreciate prestige and are willing to pay a premium for it.

5. Pricing-based positioning - This strategy emphasizes competitive pricing to create a distinct brand identity. Tech brands may position themselves as offering gadgets, hardware, or software at unbeatable prices. In the smartphone market, for example, brands like Xiaomi have built a reputation for offering high-quality smartphones at significantly lower prices compared to their competitors like Apple or Samsung. Xiaomi's strategy is to focus on providing value-driven, budget-friendly options for consumers without compromising product quality. By consistently offering competitive pricing, they have positioned themselves as an affordable yet feature-rich alternative in the highly competitive smartphone market, attracting budget-conscious consumers who prioritize cost-effectiveness.

Now let's say we have a new AI-powered smartphone we would like to launch and name it MysticAI. As part of our research, we will look at the global smartphone market data from recent years, and we will find that from 2021-2023, Samsung, Apple, and Xiaomi had the largest global market share respectively.

Global Smartphone Shipments Market Share (%)							
Brands	Q3 2021	Q4 2021	Q1 2022	Q2 2022	Q3 2022	Q4 2022	Q1 2023	Q2 2023
Samsung	20%	19%	23%	21%	21%	19%	22%	20%
Apple	14%	22%	18%	16%	16%	23%	21%	17%
Xiaomi	13%	12%	12%	13%	13%	11%	11%	12%

Source: Mobile Devices Monitor

We will then choose two key product benefits, based on what we learned is important to our target customers, and place them on a positioning map axes, which is a diagram that allows you to compare your product to the competition and identify opportunities for new products in the marketplace.

In this example, we will compare smartphones' pricing vs. quality. We will start by positioning Samsung, the leader in market share, in a large-sized circle in the high-price-high-quality quadrant (No.2) due to its relatively high prices and commendable device quality.

Next to it, we will place Apple, the second in line, in a medium-sized circle, reflecting its premium price point and perceived superior quality. Then, in the low-price-high-quality quadrant (No.3), we will set Xiaomi, holding the third-largest market share, in a slightly smaller circle, representing its affordable pricing and decent device quality. We can continue this process, adding other significant competitors as necessary.

Finally, we will decide where to position our new MysticAI smartphone based on our product features, ROI strategy, and marketing aspirations. Once we have a general positioning map visualization, we will create our unique value proposition.

Positioning Map

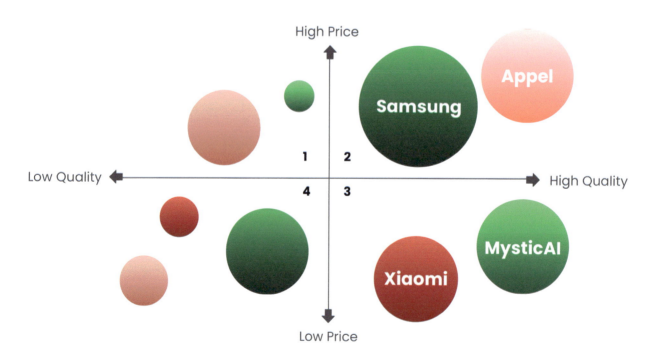

MESSAGING

A unique value proposition (UVP), also known as a unique selling proposition (USP), is a clear and concise statement that communicates the distinctive benefits a product, service, or brand offers to its target audience, setting it apart from competitors and compelling potential customers to choose it over alternatives.

It answers the fundamental question of "Why should I choose you?" by highlighting the unique, valuable, and relevant attributes that meet the specific pain points, needs, or desires of the target market. A well-crafted UVP captures the essence of what makes a product or brand exceptional and unforgettable in the eyes of customers.

A UVP statement conveys more information than a tagline or slogan, and a business typically displays it on its website homepage and social media profiles, and incorporates it into its marketing strategy.

Unique Value Proposition (UVP)

UVP – Winning Zone
Clear point of difference that meets the customer's needs

Don't Go There – Losing Zone
The competitor does it better, aim for your unfair advantages instead

Me Too – Risky
Competitive battleground, you'll have to have superior execution

Who Cares – Waste Of Time
Don't battle over areas the customer doesn't care about

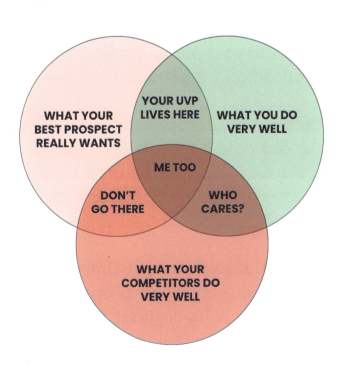

Here is an example of a unique value proposition template that can help you describe your target audience, what sets your product apart, and why customers should care about it:

UVP Template

For **[target customers]** with **[customer need/problem]** our **[company/product]** is a **[solution/category]** that uniquely solves this by **[benefit]**.

So for our new smartphone, MysticAI, our unique value proposition might look like this:

Example:

For tech-savvy professionals who desire powerful performance and an immersive user experience, the new MysticAI smartphone is a next-generation mobile device that uniquely solves this by offering ultra-fast processing speeds, an AI-driven interface, and a crystal-clear display.

There are additional product messaging types you should use to promote your brand, some of them can be a sub-version of the value proposition. Let's break down the differences:

Unique value proposition = product or service value
For example, Spotify is "A digital music, podcast, and video service that gives a million creative artists the opportunity to live off their art and billions of fans the opportunity to enjoy and be inspired by it all over the world."

Mission statement = business goal
Details your objective as an organization. For example, Google's mission statement is "To organize the world's information and make it universally accessible and useful."

Tagline = brand essence or idea

A short statement that embodies a certain aspect of your brand or business. For example, Apple's iconic "Think Different" tagline captured in two simple words Apple's vision for the company in 1997 and it continues to resonate today.

Slogan = campaign lead message

A short, catchy statement that brands use in marketing campaigns to sell a specific product. For example, Microsoft's 1994 brand advertising campaign used "Where do you want to go today?" one of the most powerful slogans that implied limitless software capabilities with equally limitless options for the user. While taglines are more permanent representations of your brand, slogans can be changed frequently and are often particular to specific campaigns.

After finalizing your positioning and messaging strategy, turn to create a marketing brief. This brief will serve as the foundation for your go-to-market plan and marketing campaigns.

Marketing Brief

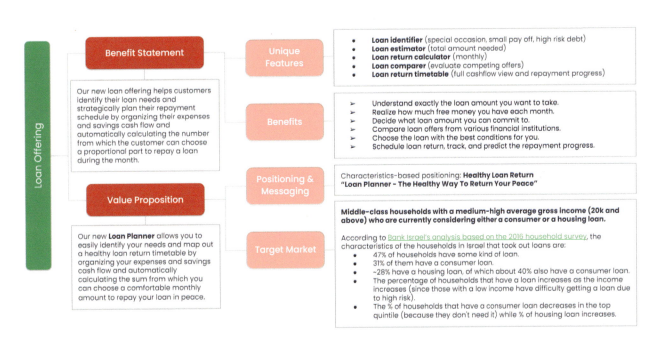

Your marketing brief should include:

- The name of your new product or service offering;

- The benefit statement, which is a written technical description that effectively conveys the core advantages of your product or service. You might begin by requesting a foundational description of the new offering from your company's product owner, and from there, you can refine it into an internal and customer-ready description for your support and knowledge endeavors;

- A unique value proposition for your marketing assets and campaigns;

- The features and benefits of your product, which you should retrieve by working closely with the product department to articulate;

- The product positioning and messaging;

- The specific target audience for your marketing initiatives.

Once your marketing brief is done, share it with your product and marketing teams to ensure alignment and turn to plan your product launch.

GO-TO-MARKET STRATEGY

A go-to-market (GTM) strategy is a step-by-step plan for launching a new product to the market or extending the reach of an existing product into a new market.

Launching a product is a big investment, and no matter how cutting-edge it is, the way you market and sell your product can make or break its success. Creating a thought-through strategy helps you ensure you take everything into account and avoid costly mistakes.

With that said, it's important to note that while a GTM strategy plays a crucial role in the successful launch and adoption of a product, a PMM has a broader set of responsibilities that encompasses the entire product lifecycle and a deeper involvement in the marketing and product strategy. Your GTM strategy draws from your long-term marketing plan, but it's tailored to a specific launch.

A well-crafted GTM strategy sets your initiative up for success by answering the following categorical questions:

- **Product-market fit:** What product are you selling, and what unique problem does it solve?

- **Target audience:** Who is your ideal customer, and what pain points do they experience?

- **Competition and demand:** Where will you sell your product, and what the demand and competition look like in those markets?

- **Distribution:** On what mediums will you sell the product, and how will you attain your target customers?

As we covered most of the steps in the previous chapters, it's now time to turn to the final step and strategize our product launch plan.

For this purpose, it's vital to map the buyer journey funnel, which is how customers go from understanding their problem to considering your product as a solution and deciding to purchase.

Buyer Journey Funnel

State of Mind

I know the product & what it has to offer

It's at the top of my mind, I'm interested in it, and I have positive associations with it

I'm considering the product and I am doing some research

I go to the website, I purchase the product

I am having a great experience with the product; I get help when I ask for it on social media and in emails

I tell everyone they should purchase the product too

Primary Tools

Content marketing, social media, paid advertising, SEO/SEM, media & PR coverage, reviews & referrals

Landing pages, one-pagers, eBooks, newsletters, case studies, retargeting

Sales pages, demos, free consultation, free trials, promotions, email marketing, support materials

Payment systems

The product, knowledge base and support guides

Reviews & referrals, user-generated content

Next, you'll need to pick your marketing channels and tools. Marketing channels are the different types of content you use to create demand for your product and move potential customers down the marketing funnel.

The marketing channels you choose depend on two factors - your target audience and the stage your potential customers are at along their buyer journey. You should use different channels for different phases of the buyer journey. Depending on where customers are in the funnel, different types of marketing content can help move them to the next phase.

You also want to ensure that the marketing channels you choose fit how your target audience consumes content. For example, if your ideal customer uses LinkedIn but not Facebook or Instagram, you may want to focus on LinkedIn posts and ads.

GOAL SETTING

Every great go-to-market strategy starts with clear objectives. Goals give you specific targets to aim for, an implicit timeline, and a way to measure progress. Without clearly defined goals it's hard to tell if your strategy is working.

Here are a few different goal-setting frameworks you can use to set measurable objectives. Depending on your business needs, you can combine these strategies or use them on their own:

- **SMART goal** - an acronym representing goals that are Specific, Measurable, Achievable, Relevant/Realistic, and Time-Bound. Defining these parameters helps ensure a clear sense of direction, steering your endeavors toward a specific destination within a defined time frame, and enables effective progress tracking.

SMART Goal

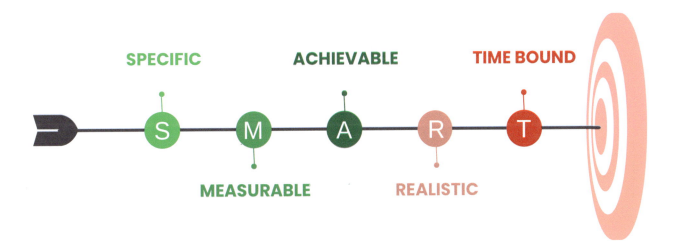

It follows this format:

Our goal is to **[quantifiable objective]** by **[timeframe or deadline]**. **[Key players or teams]** will accomplish this goal by **[what steps you'll take to achieve the goal]**. Accomplishing this goal will **[result or benefit]**.

A SMART-goal statement for a new app might look like this:

Example:

Our goal is to acquire 100,000 new app users within the first six months after launch. The marketing teams will accomplish this goal by executing targeted digital advertising campaigns, optimizing app store listings, and implementing a referral program. Accomplishing this goal will increase our user base and drive initial product adoption.

- **Key performance indicators (KPIs)** - quantitative metrics that help you track the progress toward your business objectives. Once you defined your high-level SMART goal for your overall GTM strategy, drill down and establish KPIs for the product launch. KPIs will let you know when you're on the right path to success and when you need to reassess your efforts and try again. For example, you could track total purchases and ad click-throughs and define the KPI like this:

Example:

Within 3 months, we need to generate 100K new website visitors and 1M social media followers to position our product as a leader in AI-powered customer communications.

Next, define the related activities you should take and the output metrics you should follow, which are the means of achieving those KPIs. You should also define your north star metric (NSM) for each KPI you set.

> "A north star metric (NSM) is the one measurement that's most predictive of a company's long-term success. To qualify as a "North Star", a metric must do three things: lead to revenue, reflect customer value, and measure progress."
>
> **- MixPanel**

- **Objectives and Key Results (OKRs)** - This strategy pairs the objectives you want to achieve with the key results you'll use to measure progress. It follows this format:

"I will **[objective]** as measured by **[key result]**."

Example:

The marketing team will increase awareness of a new product, as measured by the following key results: Increase social media engagement by 50%, Drive 50K web visitors to the product page, generate 5000 demo requests, and acquire 1000 new business customers.

Once you're set on your chosen goal-setting framework, illustrate the campaign strategy to ensure your marketing and product teams are aligned and everyone understands the mission of the campaign and the logic behind it.

Partners Who Save Together, Multiply Together
"Multi" Service Initiative & Campaign Goals

Our Mission
Drive more customers to add a partner to their Cashflow account in order to multiply their probability to convert to paying customers and be successful with the service.

Our "Multi" Opportunity
The new "Multi" button enables customers to add their partners to their Cashflow account immediately after signup, so they can explore the service together, connect their joint financial credentials, set collective goals, track and celebrate their saving progress during the trial period, and beyond.

⭐ Northstar: No. of monthly customers who added a partner

⭐ Metric 1: No. of monthly clicks on the "Multi" button

⭐ Metric 2: No. of monthly views of the "Multi" website's landing page

⭐ Metric 3: Total no. of clicks on the "Multi" social ad

58%
Of Total Customers Are Married

66%
Of Paying Customers Added Their Partners

2x
Better Converting Chances
Adding a partner to an account doubles the chance of converting to paying customers!

34%
More Monthly Savings
Adding a partner to an account increases the monthly savings per customer by an average of 34%!

71%
Increase In CLV
Adding a partner to an account contributes to a greater customer lifetime value by an average of 71%!

Before planning your campaign activities, it's also crucial to mind your company's marketing budget to ensure your campaign will be executed efficiently and that the ROI will be as high as you hope. For this purpose, schedule a meeting with your VP of marketing or CMO and get their final approval.

Once your manager approves the campaign budget, plan the product launch activities and allocate responsibilities to your marketing teams.

As a PMM, it's your job to own and create a high-level launch plan, ensuring that unified marketing strategy guidelines will be understood and followed before each team executes it. Be sure to set fundamentals such as target audience, key messages, competitors, goals, objectives, results, and metrics for each team and suggest relevant marketing activities and channels.

Work with your colleagues to plan the most effective ways to achieve your SMART goals, KPIs, or OKRs, and continue to serve as a guide for any adjustments that may come up as you test your marketing efforts and track the results.

High-Level Product Launch Plan

Fundamentals	Owners	Activities	Output Metrics
Purpose: Launch the new 'Loan Planner' service to the Israeli market targeting middle-class households, with a medium-high average gross income of 20k and above, who are currently considering getting either a consumer or a housing loan.	**Product Marketing**	- Product objectives & benefits - Market research & competitive analysis - Target market, personas, Jobs To Be Done - Positioning and messaging - Pricing strategy & discounts - Purchase process - Website landing page - Knowledge base section - Customer success guide	**- Northstar: Total no. of 'Loan Planner' customers** - No. of current customers who subscribed to the new service - No. of new customers who subscribed due to the new loan offering. - Total revenue from 'Loan Planner' - CLV
Objectives: - Gaining a foothold in the Israeli loan market by achieving 50% market awareness. - Registering at least 25% of current customers for the new service. - Acquiring additional 15% of new customers who will subscribe due to the new loan offering.	**Brand & Communications**	- Branding materials - Newsletter + WhatsApp Msgs - Organic social media posts - Community engagement - Influencer partnerships - Launch webinar/conference - PR & media relations	- Organic traffic (views, clicks, comments, shares, followers) - No. of leads acquired at the launch events.
Style & Tone: Healthy, safe, peaceful, economical, easy, smart. **Example:** "Loan Planner - The Healthy Way To Return Your Peace"	**Growth**	- Paid social media campaigns: LinkedIn, Facebook, Instagram, Google, YouTube - Referral links distribution & link building - User cycles tracking & optimization (acquisition, retention, activation, renewal, cancellation) - SEO	- Landing page conversion rates. - Social media conversion rates. - Newsletter/Msgs conversion rates. - Referrals conversion rates. - CPL (Cost Per Lead). - CAC (Customer Acquisition Cost).
Competitors: 1. _____ 2. _____ 3. _____	**Content**	- Promotional + explanatory videos - Blog & PR articles - Case studies & reports - SEO	- Organic traffic (views, clicks, comments, shares, followers).

Finally, schedule a GTM timeline and make sure each team is aware of the time constraints and committed to delivering results within that timeframe, as everyone needs to contribute and work together to make the launch a success. It is also vital that you schedule weekly meetings with the leader of each team to answer any questions, address needs, and ensure that everyone is aligned and delivers the desired results on time.

GTM Timeline

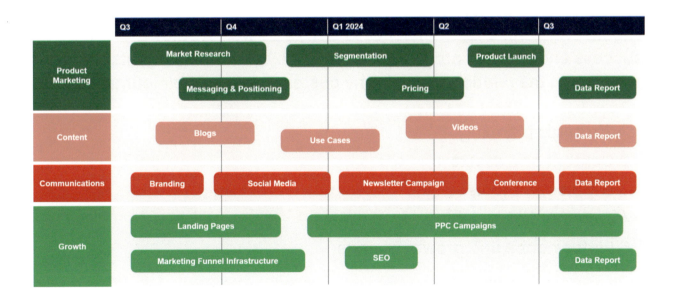

SALES & CUSTOMER SUCCESS ENABLEMENT

Product marketing's role is to educate marketing, product, salespeople, and customer success on the target audience, market segments, buyer personas, customer needs, and product offerings. One aspect of this role is sales enablement. Putting the relevant sales enablement plans in place is critical in helping your sales reps optimize their performance and generate revenue.

> **"Sales enablement is the process of empowering a sales team with the right knowledge, skills, and collateral, so they can help them effectively sell the product to prospective customers and close more deals."**
>
> **– Product Marketing Alliance**

In addition, as the buyer journey doesn't start or end with a sale, PMMs should empower customer success teams as well. A sales and customer success enablement program includes five essential elements that help strengthen the relationship with the customer along their journey:

1. Strategic planning
2. Content and assets
3. Enablement tools
4. Training and coaching
5. Performance and growth metrics

Let's delve into each of these stages.

1. Strategic planning

The goal of your GTM strategy is to sell your product, so it's essential to decide how you'll sell to your target audience and turn prospective customers into buyers. That's where your sales strategy comes in. Here are the four most common sales strategies. As needed, you can combine these strategies to fit your specific product and business model.

- **Self-service model:** The customers purchase your product on their own. This is a common sales process for e-commerce, in which customers can find and buy products online. While this option doesn't require a dedicated sales team, you need to invest in marketing to drive traffic to your website.

- **Inside sales model:** The sales team nurtures prospective customers to convince them to purchase your product. This is a good option for products with a medium price point that is a bit more complex, like design software for teams.

- **Field sales model:** The salespeople focus on closing big enterprise deals. This option requires more sales investment and a longer sales cycle, but there's a big payoff. For example, you might use a field sales model to sell enterprise resource planning (ERP) software to large companies.

- **Channel model:** External partners sell your product for you. While this option gives you less say in how you market your product, it's the cheapest option and can work well if you partner with companies that sell similar products. For example, if you're selling an automotive IoT device, you could partner with an automotive parts supplier.

2. Content and assets

Sales enablement assets come in various forms, serving as a company's strategic tools tailored to its product, industry, and market. These assets play a crucial role in advancing organizations towards their ultimate objectives.

Here are some paramount sales enablement assets at your disposal:

- **Sales one-pagers:** As the name suggests, these single-page documents offer a quick overview of your business, team, service, or product, making it easy to grasp and share with prospects.

- **Battlecards:** These concise documents provide your sales team with vital insights into a competitor's strategy, key sales messages, product details, and value propositions to give you an edge in the market.

- **Sales scripts:** You can also equip your team with well-crafted scripts that offer talking points and guidance to navigate challenging scenarios with ease.

- **Product sheets:** When your sales team needs to dive into the technical aspects of a product or service, product sheets serve as handy references, ensuring they have the information they need at their fingertips.

- **Knowledgebase and support guides:** In addition, it's important to note that many product marketing managers, especially in cases where a dedicated knowledge manager or technical writer is not on board, are in charge of creating the knowledgebase and support guides. These technical materials play a pivotal role in assisting both your sales and customer success teams, serving potential buyers during the product research phase, and helping existing customers while using the product. To ensure customer satisfaction and retention, it's essential to maintain accessible and comprehensive guides that cater to leads, prospects, and current customers throughout their buyer journey.

Battlecard

Solution Overview
Lorem ipsum dolor sit amet, consectetur adipiscing elit. Cras arcu purus, efficitur in ante et, ultrices.

Requirements To Meet
Lorem ipsum dolor sit amet, consectetur adipiscing elit. Cras arcu purus, efficitur in ante et, ultrices.

FAQs/Answers

Q: Quisque vulputate volutpat?
A: Nam ullamcorper turpis sed diam laoreet gravida.

Q: Quisque vulputate volutpat?
A: Nam ullamcorper turpis sed diam laoreet gravida.

Q: Quisque vulputate volutpat?
A: Nam ullamcorper turpis sed diam laoreet gravida.

Key Target Audience
Lorem ipsum dolor sit amet, consectetur adipiscing elit. Cras arcu purus, efficitur in ante et, ultrices.

Competitive Differentiation
Lorem ipsum dolor sit amet, consectetur adipiscing elit. Cras arcu purus, efficitur in ante et, ultrices.

Customer Gains
- Lorem ipsum dolor sit amet.
- Consectetur adipiscing elit.
- Cras arcu purus ultrices.

Customer Pain Points
- Lorem ipsum dolor sit amet.
- Consectetur adipiscing elit.
- Cras arcu purus ultrices.

Plan Options and Pricing

Plan	Benefits	Price
Platinum		
Gold		
Silver		

Examples: How To / Not To Engage
Lorem ipsum dolor sit amet, consectetur adipiscing elit. Cras arcu purus, efficitur in ante et, ultrices interdum nulla. Nulla magna augue, sodales at condimentum vitae, interdum non nulla. Quisque vulputate volutpat malesuada. Nam ullamcorper turpis sed diam laoreet gravida. Praesent dapibus diam non neque facilisis suscipit. Donec aliquam euismod nisi, in blandit mi facilisis a. Praesent tristique a orci non cursus. Sed sit amet pulvinar eros, non mollis nulla. Proin laoreet enim in.

3. Enablement tools

Whether your company is a three-person endeavor or a large enterprise, having the right tools, platforms, and systems is essential for effective product and service sales. These enablement tools provide crucial customer data, empowering data-driven decision-making and creating a well-informed team. They bridge the gap between marketing, sales, and customer success throughout the product lifecycle, and enable content performance tracking from creation to presentation. For example, customer relationship management (CRM) systems offer features like live chat, meeting scheduling, and email tracking, while sales intelligence software analyzes interactions between sales reps and prospects or customers, such as calls, emails, and web conferencing. Countless innovative tools provide valuable insights to help optimize conversion and overall sales and customer success performance, which product marketers can leverage to improve their enablement efforts.

4. Training and coaching

In this stage, the PMM needs to help develop a sales engagement process for the sales team to follow to add structure to their sales strategy. This is with the hope that the sales cycle runs more smoothly and ends in a closed deal. You'll need to collaborate with the head of your sales department to schedule proper times to coach your sales team and ensure they are fully equipped and informed of all the latest updates on your new product offerings so they can close bigger and better deals. Your training program should include the following stages:

- **Preparation:** Gather the sales team to see how the sales engagement process should be approached.

- **Prospecting and research:** Take the time to identify prospective customers, research them to build strong personas, and add them to the database, just like you learned in the previous chapter on customer profiles.

- **First contact:** This is the outreach stage but it shouldn't be focused on closing a deal. This is to nurture potential relationships with prospective customers, teach them about the company's product or service, and get that initial link of interest.

- **Lead nurturing:** This is where you begin to develop those relationships with the customers you first reached out to, with the hope of leading them through the sales process and getting a closed deal. You can do this through follow-up calls or emails, answering any questions they may have, and supporting them. Hence, they feel more comfortable and connected with your organization and solution.

- **Closing the deal:** Hopefully, the first four stages have been successful by now, and you should be moving on to closing the deal with your prospective customer. It's important that this entire process isn't forced, and that both ends are feeling happy with the deal that has occurred. This leaves the potential for a longer relationship between both parties.

5. Performance and growth metrics

Finally, the success of a sales enablement program should be measured by examining uplifts in productivity, win rates, and revenue growth, and it's recommended that you use one of the goal-setting and measurement methods you learned in the previous chapter of this guide to track them effectively.

For this stage, I suggest you schedule a meeting with your head of sales, the chief revenue officer (CRO), and your CEO, if available, to strategize your goals and set concrete revenue targets that will align with your company's overall growth plan, including time and financial constraints.

Performance and Growth Metrics

SOLUTIONS TO COMMON DISPUTES

COMMONLY DISPUTED PMM RESPONSIBILITIES

Certain responsibilities often spark debate about whether or not a PMM should own them. Here are the most commonly disputed ones:

- Pricing
- Content Development
- Product Feature Suggestions
- Product User Journey Optimization
- Product Communication

We'll now explore each one to determine who should ideally own these responsibilities in a high-tech company.

PRICING

Amongst the most disputed PMM responsibilities, pricing is the one that, in my opinion, shouldn't even be up for debate. This is because pricing is an essential aspect of product marketing, and it should ideally be owned first and foremost by the PMM in the company for several reasons:

- **Product expertise:** PMMs are typically the experts on the product and its value proposition. They understand the product features, benefits, and competitive positioning. This knowledge is crucial when determining the right pricing strategy.

- **Market knowledge:** PMMs possess a deep understanding of the target market, buyer personas, and customer needs. They are well-equipped to assess market conditions and trends that directly influence pricing decisions.

- **Competitive intelligence:** PMMs continuously monitor the competitive landscape. They track competitors' pricing strategies, helping the company position its products effectively and set competitive pricing.

- **Aligning pricing with value:** PMMs can ensure that pricing aligns with the perceived value of the product. They can communicate the product's unique value proposition to justify the chosen price point.

- **Customer insights:** PMMs often gather direct customer feedback and insights. This information is invaluable for setting prices that resonate with the target audience and adjusting them to specific buyer journey stages and campaigns.

With that said, while PMMs are ideally suited to lead pricing efforts, they should work collaboratively with other teams, including sales, product management, and finance, to ensure that pricing decisions align with the company's growth goals and constraints. Skilled PMMs dedicate their time to collaborating with these teams, guaranteeing a unified approach to pricing.

The bottom line is when it comes to the pricing ownership battle, the winner is the PMM, hands down.

COST, MARGIN & MARKUP

Before we go over the different pricing strategies, it's crucial to understand the roles played by cost, margin, and markup. Let's delve into the definition of each:

- **Cost:** Also known as cost of goods sold (COGS), it pertains to the expenses related to manufacturing, sourcing, or creating your product. It encompasses the costs of materials, labor, payments to suppliers, and any losses incurred. However, it doesn't include overhead and operational expenses like marketing, advertising, maintenance, or bills.

- **Margin (specifically gross margin):** This represents the amount your business earns once you deduct the COGS.

- **Markup:** This denotes the additional amount you charge for your product beyond the COGS.

Now, let's explore some common pricing strategies. These strategies can often be combined when determining the prices for your products and services.

PRICING STRATEGIES

Oftentimes, organizations treat pricing as a secondary consideration when introducing a new product when it should be a primary focus in their decision-making process, as one of the initial considerations for a customer when deciding to purchase your product is its price.

The price point defines the product value and can significantly influence the customer's purchasing decisions. PMMs should be well-versed in various pricing strategies to select the most suitable strategy for each one of their products.

"A pricing strategy is an approach used by a company to determine the appropriate price for its product or service, aiming to optimize sales volume and market share while considering buyer preferences and market trends."

These strategies vary based on a company's nature and specific circumstances, making teaching them challenging because there is no one universal solution. This is why it's crucial to conduct market research and select the most suitable pricing strategy for your solution, as your target audience will respond differently to different prices, depending on their affordability and the pricing strategies used by other businesses in the market.

A successful pricing strategy should strike a balance between affordability for your target audience and covering various expenses, including manufacturing costs and employee salaries. Discovering the optimal pricing strategy for your product will not only attract customers and boost sales but also ensure cost coverage and, ultimately, generate the desired profits.

There are several pricing strategies you can consider, and we will now review the most common ones:

- **Competitor-based pricing**

This strategy uses competitors' pricing as a benchmark, aligning your product's price with others in the market. It's especially useful in highly competitive markets where even a slight price difference can influence customers' decisions. For instance, if you're selling project management software and similar products in the market are priced between $20 and $40 per month, a competitor-based pricing strategy would position your software's price within that range to remain competitive or slightly below your competition to attract customers exploring different project management solutions.

Moreover, it's essential to understand that customers are primarily seeking the best value, which doesn't always mean the lowest price. This approach is particularly effective when your business offers something unique that competitors don't, such as exceptional customer service, a generous return policy, or exclusive loyalty rewards.

- **Cost-plus pricing**

This strategy centers on the COGS of your product or service. It's also called markup pricing because it entails marking up products to achieve desired profit margins. To apply this approach, you add a fixed percentage to the production cost of your product. For example, let's say you're in the business of IoT devices. If the cost of manufacturing an IoT device is $50 per unit, and your target profit per sale is $20, you would set the price at $70, reflecting a 40% markup.

This pricing strategy is commonly employed by retailers dealing with physical products. However, it might not be the most suitable option for service-based or SaaS companies, as their products often offer significantly greater value than the cost of production.

Cost-plus pricing is effective when your competitors are utilizing a similar pricing model. However, it may not be the best approach for customer acquisition if your competitors are prioritizing customer growth over maximizing profits. Therefore, before implementing this strategy, it's crucial to conduct a comprehensive pricing analysis, including an assessment of your closest competitors, to ensure that this approach aligns with your specific objectives.

- **Dynamic pricing**

Also referred to as surge pricing, demand pricing, or time-based pricing, is a flexible pricing approach that adjusts prices in response to market conditions and customer demand. Various industries, such as hotels, airlines, event venues, and eCommerce companies, utilize dynamic pricing by leveraging algorithms that factor in competitor pricing, demand fluctuations, and other relevant variables. These algorithms empower companies to adapt their prices to align with customers' willingness to pay at the precise moment they decide to make a purchase.

A prominent example of dynamic pricing in the software industry is the pricing strategy employed by ride-sharing platforms like Uber and Lyft. These companies adjust their ride fares in real time based on various factors, such as demand, traffic conditions, and the availability of drivers. When demand is high or during peak hours, ride prices increase, while they decrease when demand is lower.

Dynamic pricing can serve as a valuable tool in your marketing strategy. It allows your team to proactively plan promotions and configure pricing algorithms to launch promotional prices at optimal times. Additionally, you can conduct real-time A/B testing of dynamic pricing to optimize your profitability.

- **High-low pricing**

With this strategy, a company initially introduces a product at a premium price but later reduces the price when the product becomes less novel or relevant. It is often associated with discounts, clearance sales, and end-of-season promotions, which is why it is also referred to as discount pricing. In this method, a product's price alternates between "high" and "low" over a given period. This strategy can help maintain consistent traffic on your website or stores throughout the year.

High-low pricing is commonly employed by retail businesses dealing with seasonal goods or products that experience frequent changes, such as smartphones, fashion, home decor, and furniture. What makes this strategy attractive to sellers is that consumers enjoy the anticipation of sales and discounts, which is why events like Black Friday and other universal discount days are so popular.

- **Skimming pricing**

This strategy involves setting the highest possible price for a new product and gradually reducing it over time as its popularity diminishes. Unlike high-low pricing, this approach features a gradual and extended reduction of prices. It is commonly used for tech products like video game consoles and smartphones as they become less relevant. Skimming pricing helps recover initial costs and continue selling products beyond their initial novelty. However, it can potentially frustrate early buyers who bought the product at full price.

Apple, for example, employs a skimming pricing strategy when it launches a new iPhone model. When the iPhone is released, it comes at a premium price, attracting early adopters who are willing to pay more for the latest features. As time passes and newer models are introduced, Apple gradually reduces the prices of older iPhone versions. This approach allows Apple to cater to a diverse range of customers, from those seeking the latest technology to budget-conscious buyers, ensuring their products remain attractive and accessible throughout the product lifecycle.

Skimming pricing can be effective for products with varying lifecycles. Products with a short lifecycle require quick profit generation in the early stages, while those with longer lifecycles can maintain higher prices for an extended period. This approach allows more effective marketing management without the constant need for price adjustments across all products.

- **Penetration pricing**

In contrast to skimming pricing, this strategy involves entering the market with a significantly lower price to divert attention and revenue away from higher-priced competitors. This approach is typically applied for a limited time and works well for new startups seeking customers or established companies entering competitive markets. It is a disruptive strategy that may result in short-term losses, with the hope of retaining initial customers as prices eventually rise.

- **Loss leader pricing**

Here, retailers offer intentionally low-priced items to attract customers and boost sales of higher-priced products. This approach can lead to sustained revenue and business growth if it is supported by value and excellent products or services. When using this strategy, emphasize the value of your offerings and position price as a secondary consideration.

- **Value-based pricing**

This strategy adapts product prices to match different customer segments' perceptions of value, and the price is set based on customer interest and data. This approach results in varying prices for different customers or segments. Just be sure that your audiences are distinct enough in what they are willing to pay for.

Using a value-based pricing approach, let's assume customers have different preferences regarding ad interruptions. Research shows that some customers are willing to pay extra to have an ad-free experience. Those who don't mind ads may prefer a lower price point.

Take, for example, Netflix and Hulu, both offering on-demand streaming of movies and TV shows. They present a subscription tier with limited ads and another without ads at a higher price. This value-based approach enables them to cater to customers' preferences. By setting the ad-free version at a slightly higher price, they reflect the added value of uninterrupted streaming. In this way, both services employ value-based pricing to align with customers' preferences and enhance their perceived value.

The primary drawback of this strategy is the time investment. Value-based pricing demands more time and resources for market research and segmentation compared to other methods. Yet, as the saying goes, if it's worth doing, it's worth doing well.

- **Psychological pricing**

This strategy leverages human psychology to enhance your sales. For instance, the "9-digit effect" illustrates how a product priced at $99.99 may be perceived as a better deal compared to a $100 product simply because of the presence of the number "9" in the price.

Another psychological pricing tactic involves situating a higher-priced item next to the one you intend to sell either in-store or online. You can also employ offers like "buy one, get one 50% off (or free)" to create a sense of opportunity too good to resist.

Furthermore, adjusting the font, size, and color of your pricing information in and around your products has, in numerous cases, demonstrated the ability to boost sales. Effectively implementing a psychological pricing strategy requires a deep understanding of your target market. To achieve optimal results, tailor your marketing to match your customers' preferences. If your audience values discounts and coupons, catering to this desire can tap into their psychological need to save money. Conversely, if your customers prioritize quality and are willing to pay a premium for it, focusing solely on having the lowest price might not align with your sales goals. Your pricing strategies should align with the motivations that drive your customers' purchasing decisions.

- **Geographic pricing**

This strategy involves setting different prices for products or services based on their geographical location or the specific market they are sold in. This approach may be employed when selling to customers from different countries or regions with variations in economic conditions or wage levels.

Effectively marketing products or services with geographically based pricing is made simpler with the help of paid social media advertising. By segmenting your advertising based on zip codes, cities, or regions, you can achieve accurate results at a reasonable cost. This strategy ensures that your pricing remains consistent even as specific customers travel or relocate, helping you manage your marketing expenses more efficiently.

PRICING MODELS

Your company's pricing strategy sets the stage for how you determine prices across different product lines. Now let's explore various models of pricing tactics tailored to the tech industry:

1. Freemium pricing

This model is a blend of "free" and "premium" which offers a basic product version for free to entice users to upgrade or access additional features for a fee. This model is popular among software-as-a-service companies, also known as SaaS. With freemium pricing, prices should align with the perceived value of the product. They should be accessible, ensuring users can transition to paid versions smoothly as they gain more features and benefits.

While freemium pricing may not generate immediate revenue, it provides valuable access to potential paying customers. You can nurture these leads over time, leveraging their contact information to create brand loyalty. Freemium users also provide various user insights about your product that you can leverage to improve your offerings while your customer pool grows.

2. Premium pricing

On the other hand, premium pricing, also known as prestige or luxury pricing, positions products at a high price point to convey a sense of value, luxury, or exclusivity. It focuses on perceived value rather than production costs. Prestige pricing is closely tied to brand perception and awareness. Companies using this model are known for delivering status and value, justifying higher prices. Marketing premium-priced tech products relies on influencing the perception of your brand as luxurious within the market. Tactics include leveraging influencers, controlling supply, and boosting demand.

3. Subscription pricing

This strategy is prevalent in the tech industry, offering monthly or tiered subscriptions for SaaS products, mobile apps, and more, and it ensures predictable recurring revenue. However, while subscription pricing offers steady income, it may face customer churn. That is why this method should be accompanied by effective customer retention strategies. In addition, when marketing subscription products buyer personas segmentation helps cater to each tier's needs and preferences. Creating differentiation within your subscription offerings can enhance appeal and retention.

4. Hourly pricing

This model is common among consultants, freelancers, and laborers, and values time as a direct exchange for money. While some clients may hesitate to adopt this model, it can reward efficiency for high-volume projects. For businesses with quick, high-volume projects, hourly pricing can attract customers seeking cost-effective, short-term commitments, making it an attractive option.

5. Project-based pricing

In contrast to hourly pricing, project-based pricing charges a flat fee per project, independent of time. It is also commonly used by consultants, freelancers, and laborers. Highlighting the benefits of working on a project basis can make this pricing strategy more appealing, focusing on the project's outcome rather than the hours invested.

At Fiverr, for example, sellers can create Gigs and choose their starting price point. They can even take this a step further and offer Gig Packages to buyers. These contain multiple price ranges, and sellers can offer various tailored service packages. This way, buyers can pick and choose their desired offer per their particular requirements.

6. Bundle pricing

This brings us to the bundle pricing model, which involves packaging complementary products or services together and selling them as a single package or individually. This approach adds value and encourages customers to purchase multiple products upfront. Marketing bundled deals can increase sales by enticing customers with added value and cost savings, making it a smart strategy for upselling and cross-selling.

Now, let's turn to building your own customized pricing plan.

PRICING CONSIDERATIONS

When selecting a pricing plan, there's no one-size-fits-all solution as your choice depends on your unique circumstances. Pricing plans are essential for maintaining a healthy cash flow, but you need absolute clarity on several key factors:

1. Production costs: Understand the cost of manufacturing your product or offering your service.

2. Client value: Determine your product or service value to clients. What problem are you solving for them, and what's that worth?

3. Customer budget: Know your customers' financial capabilities and their willingness to spend money on a solution.

4. Operational expenses: Consider the overall running costs of your business.

5. Immediate financial obligations: Identify critical short-term costs like loan repayments that must be covered.

6. Competitor pricing: Research how your competitors are pricing similar products or services.

To maximize your profit, your pricing plan should take all these factors into account. It might even necessitate a thorough review of your overall business plan, potentially involving brand development, team restructuring, and more. Keep in mind that pricing strategies and models aren't set in stone. Regularly assess your plan and be ready to adapt when things don't go as expected. Metrics like sales figures and churn rates can guide your decision-making process.

VALUABLE PRICING LESSONS

To sum up, Silvia Kiely Frucci, a product marketing expert, shares these valuable pricing lessons:

1. **Be flexible:** While you should follow a pricing process, don't feel constrained by it.

2. **Team effort:** Pricing decisions are often most effective when made collaboratively.

3. **Perfect pricing is a myth:** Understand that there's no one-size-fits-all pricing structure.

4. **Negative price testing:** Experimenting with different prices can help you re-evaluate your product's value proposition.

5. **Pricing beyond numbers:** Pricing is more than just setting a number; it's also about understanding your market and customer needs.

ITERATION AND OPTIMIZATION

Above all, remember that pricing is not a one-time decision but an ongoing process. Rarely will you hit the perfect price right away. It may require a few attempts and plenty of research, and that's perfectly normal. PMMs can continually assess pricing performance and adjust as needed to optimize revenue and profitability.

CONTENT DEVELOPMENT

According to a global survey of more than 2000 PMMs conducted by Product Marketing Alliance in 2020, a staggering 93.7% reported being accountable for generating sales content within their organizations. This trend was similarly reflected in my Tech PMM Responsibilities 2023 Survey, conducted within the largest PMM community in Israel.

However, it seems there's a certain level of confusion between top-of-the-funnel content, which is primarily owned by content managers, and mid-bottom-of-the-funnel content, which should be owned and strategized by the PMM, with opportunities for collaboration with content managers in its execution.

Top-of-the-funnel content refers to inbound marketing content that helps attract website traffic and convert visitors into leads, and mid-of-the-funnel content refers to content that communicates the functionality and benefits of your product or services. Finally, the bottom-of-the-funnel content enables your sales team to sell effectively.

Top-Bottom Content Funnel

Content Managers

Product Marketing & Content Managers

Product Marketing & Content Managers

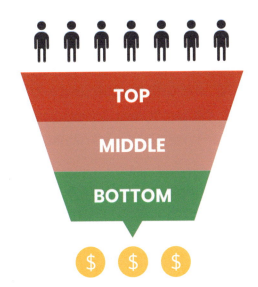

PRODUCT MARKETING-LED CONTENT

Product marketing-led content is a potent tool when executed correctly, serving as a means to inform and influence target audiences. To ensure your content reaches these audiences through various marketing channels, it's essential to craft engaging materials in diverse formats tailored to their interests and needs:

1. Product pages: Product marketers typically manage the website's product pages. These pages should highlight your various product and service offerings and provide the information that prospects need to conduct product research and understand what you sell.

2. Product videos: Videos can be a great way to communicate how your products work and how they help your potential customers, particularly for products that lend themselves to a more visual explanation. They're also great for giving site visitors a quick overview of what you offer as well as providing deeper dives into specific product features and use cases. Well-designed and visually captivating videos are extremely efficient for marketing products, easily shareable, and can enhance engagement, especially when accompanied by subtitles.

3. Product blog category: While the company blog is primarily owned by content managers and includes inbound marketing content such as thought leadership and educational articles to attract visitors, it's equally beneficial to maintain a dedicated product blog category. This specialized category can serve as a platform for sharing product updates and important company announcements. Using this category, you can effectively communicate significant product, service, and feature enhancements, along with notable corporate news. Additionally, it's acceptable to occasionally integrate subtle product mentions into your main blog content.

4. eBooks: eBooks serve as comprehensive, long-form content that can be compiled from existing articles or developed from scratch. Offering valuable information to your target audience showcases your brand's industry expertise, reinforcing the value of your products.

5. Infographics: Visually appealing infographics are excellent for presenting complex information in an eye-catching manner. Infographics can be integrated into articles, white papers, and your company's social media, offering the potential for sharing and boosting brand awareness.

6. Case studies and testimonials: Demonstrating credibility is paramount in product marketing. This can be achieved through client testimonials or case studies that illustrate results achieved for clients, providing solid evidence to support any claims made.

7. ROI reports: To demonstrate the value of your solutions, regularly compile ROI reports based on customer success data. These reports showcase the positive impact of your products or services. You can create them by analyzing accessible customer data or surveying your customers about the results they've achieved.

8. Webinars: Whether live or on-demand, webinars present opportunities to feature guest brands with industry expertise, benefiting both them and your audience, thus supporting your product marketing efforts.

9. Group product demos: Consider hosting webinars that feature live group product demos, especially if your business is in the software industry. These group demos are not only a time-saver but also serve as excellent product marketing collateral. They can be promoted to both marketing leads and those with whom your sales team is actively engaged. Additionally, if you record these live demos, you can repurpose them as product demo videos on your website.

10. Product awareness surveys: Inbound marketers often attract new visitors with industry-related, top-of-the-funnel content. However, this content may not always directly address your products. To gauge what your audience thinks about your offerings, consider conducting product awareness surveys. This approach helps your product marketing team measure the effectiveness of their efforts in building awareness over time. You can send the survey to a segment of your leads or add it to your website thank-you pages to collect responses after an inquiry or purchase.

11. Sales presentations: PMMs are the primary owners of creating and maintaining sales presentations that reflect the best positioning and selling points of your various products, services, and features, particularly when new additions are introduced. The other sales enablement content assets are discussed previously in the sales enablement chapter.

12. Product digest emails: Product marketers play a crucial role in internal marketing, acting as intermediaries between the product management team and the rest of the company. Sending regular product digest emails is an effective way to share news and information about new product features and sales enablement content with the marketing, sales, and customer success teams. These emails should include essential updates and links to resources such as how-to-sell pages. Consider extending this communication to benefit the entire company, as many employees might find value in staying informed about product marketing developments.

At the heart of your product marketing content strategy lies a well-planned content calendar that facilitates content creation, publication scheduling, and synchronization across multiple marketing channels. Creating content and video strategy worksheets can help you plan and collaborate with the content department effectively.

In summary, content development can be categorized into two main segments:

1. Top-of-the-funnel inbound marketing content: This content is primarily responsible for attracting leads and is typically owned and managed by content managers.

2. Mid-bottom-of-the-funnel product marketing content: The ownership of this content falls under the purview of the PMM within the company. Collaboration with the content team is essential to effectively convey the product's key selling points and boost sales efforts.

It is also recommended that all employees contribute to content development to position the company as a thought leader in its field.

PRODUCT FEATURE SUGGESTIONS

In some tech companies, there is a blurred line between product marketing and product management, which often results in the placement of product marketing managers in the product department, while their natural most effective placement is in the marketing department, where they can strategize marketing programs with their fellow marketers.

Product marketing managers (PMMs) play a central part in bringing products to market, focusing on positioning, messaging, and sales conversion strategies. In contrast, product managers (PMs) are responsible for creating the product, concentrating on its vision, strategy, and development to ensure it meets market needs.

Despite their distinct roles, PMMs and PMs collaborate closely, sharing a common customer-centric focus, not just on the go-to-market but on the product strategy too.

PMM VALUE IN PRODUCT DEVELOPMENT

- **Maintain product alignment with market demands and its competitive positioning**

Product marketing is pivotal at the intersection of market dynamics and product offerings. Unlike PMs who shape the product, PMMs contribute insights rooted in a deep understanding of the market landscape and competition. This understanding becomes a potent tool when suggesting new features and refining existing ones, as it helps maintain product alignment with market demands and its competitive positioning.

- **Bridge the gap between technical product aspects and customer needs**

PMMs ensure the product's unique value proposition aligns with the customer's pain points. This positions PMMs as advocates for the end user. They are also in charge of identifying the product's buyer personas which they can leverage to initiate appropriate product features to match their special needs. Together with the PMs, they create a comprehensive understanding of the customer and product that enriches the decision-making process. This collaboration fosters an environment where the strengths of each role are utilized to develop a well-rounded product that satisfies both customer requirements and technical standards.

- **Ensure product alignment with the broader marketing narrative**

The synergy between PMMs and PMs is particularly valuable when considering the different lenses through which they view the product. PMMs ensure effective communication of the product's value proposition to the target audience in various stages of the buyer journey including acquisition, activation, retention, renewal, and cancellation, and can assist with onboarding, satisfying, and surveying users through various features that require storytelling or research skills. By actively participating in feature suggestions and employing well-targeted messaging tailored to different buyer personas, PMMs guarantee that product development aligns seamlessly with the overarching marketing narrative, thereby enhancing the overall customer experience throughout the user journey.

To sum up, product managers' collaboration with product marketing managers enhances their ability to make informed decisions based on a holistic market and customer understanding. To facilitate effective collaboration, PMs and PMMs engage in clear communication, regular cross-functional meetings, and shared success metrics.

Establishing a partnership built on transparency and understanding is crucial to navigating the complexities of product development. By seamlessly working together, they can harness their complementary skills to drive successful product development, contributing to the overall success of the product in the market.

Though PMs own the product strategy and roadmap, leveraging PMMs' market knowledge and understanding of the various customer needs to suggest new features and enhance existing ones contributes to building a product that aligns with market demands, strengthens the overall product strategy, and generates more revenue.

PRODUCT USER JOURNEY OPTIMIZATION

We are in the midst of a massive shift in the way people use and buy software. Today, the market is flooded with software products that cater to both B2B and B2C audiences, leading customers to demand products that are not only functional but also more aesthetic, intuitive, powerful, and cost-effective than those they used in the past.

In response to heightened expectations and growing competition, software companies are adapting their product strategies to align with customer demands and foster product growth. This evolution has given rise to a novel role – the Growth Product Manager.

> "Growth product management (GPM), refers to increasing an existing product's value and user base. Unlike traditional product management, which focuses on managing all activities required to bring a profitable product to market, growth product management aims to help an existing product become more successful."
>
> - airfocus

Growth product management is centered around refining a product through data-driven insights and optimizing the product user journey. In this approach, growth product managers (GPMs) leverage data to identify areas for improvement, potentially revising functions or features to enhance overall value. The goal is to ensure users derive maximum value from the product, leading to improved retention rates and increased referrals.

It's crucial to note that the responsibility for optimizing the product user journey lies with product managers and, when present, growth product managers—not with product marketing managers, as some might mistakenly assume.

User Journey Optimization Map

User Journey: Current State	Awareness >	Research >	Sign-Up >	Trial >	Subscription Offering
What is the customer thinking or feeling?	Not very stressed but want to save more money 😟	Realize they need a product or service to help them save more money 🙂	Curios and want to see if the service is suitable for their needs before sharing any financial information 🤔	Feel confident enough to share financial information and start managing their money better 🤓	Finish the trial and consider whether it is worth paying 45 NIS per month for the service or not 🧐
What is the customer's action?	Looking for educational content to help them diagnose their financial problem and find potential solutions	Begin to compare brands and their offerings	Join the service via the website > answer 4 questions > add personal details > confirm terms > arrive to the main screen	Add a bank account/credit card > Start a free 1-month trial > engage with the service daily	Agree to pay and add their credit card credentials - or - quit the service
What is the customer's touchpoint with the business?	* Social Media * Search Engines	* Facebook Group * Website	* Website * Cashflow Web View * Cashflow Mobile View * WhatsApp ChatBot * Email	* Cashflow Mobile View * WhatsApp ChatBot * Email	* Cashflow Mobile View * WhatsApp ChatBot * Email
What do we want to change about this step?	* Make financial terms and best practices more accessible * Reach the customers who are ready to be educated	* Improve the presentation of the service (it's not a mobile app but a web view + chat) * Demonstrate the service experience better before signing up	* Refine the switch between desktop and mobile * Let the customer understand what they'll be getting if they share their financial information	* Make it clear when the trial actually starts and ends * Make it clear where the payment details are added	* Make sure the customers have a sense of empowerment * Let the customers see what their potential saving would be if they continue with the service
How and/or why will we make this change?	* Build a financial wiki * Offer free/discounted financial courses and webinars * Create partnerships with financial advisors	* Improve the value proposition * Create a video that covers the entire flow * Create more how-to articles and guides	* Improve communications * Improve UI/UX - add categories and demo charts with no data	* Add a trial progress bar * Add a payment gateway page	* Send small wins reminders and mark the actions that the customers did well * Add insights based on customers like them

I encountered this misconception firsthand during an interview for a product marketing manager position that incorporated a growth product management skills review. Also, the confusion appears more prevalent in product-led growth (PLG) companies compared to sales-led growth (SLG) or marketing-led growth (MLG) companies.

> "Product-led growth (PLG) is a business methodology in which user acquisition, expansion, conversion, and retention are all driven primarily by the product itself. It creates company-wide alignment across teams—from engineering to sales and marketing—around the product as the largest source of sustainable, scalable business growth."
>
> - PLG Collective

That said, for successful implementation, GPMs need to actively collaborate with various teams, including PMMs. This collaborative approach ensures that the recommended changes yield positive outcomes. Without seamless communication putting ideas and strategies into action may face unnecessary challenges. Regular and transparent communication becomes essential to foster a harmonious and productive growth process.

PRODUCT COMMUNICATION

Product communication refers to all the communications that help users experience the product value. For example, in-app messages, push notifications, SMS, and product emails. An efficient product communication strategy helps users overcome feature blindness and improves their confidence in using your product to drive adoption and retention.

It's important to distinguish product communication from marketing communication, which refers to promotional campaigns, marketing channels, messages, and media that marketers use to communicate with customers along their buyer journey.

In this context, a significant debate revolves around the ownership and creation of product communication. To explore this further, I conducted an additional survey with product marketing managers and product managers to identify the most suitable position for the task. The responses, as anticipated, varied. However, 46% of the 41 votes leaned towards the PMM, with the PM receiving 34%, the UX Writer at 12%, and other marketing functions at 8% combined.

Product Communications Ownership Survey 2023

This refers to communications that derive from interactions with an app/SaaS, such as in-app messages, push notifications, SMS, and product emails (not marketing communications).

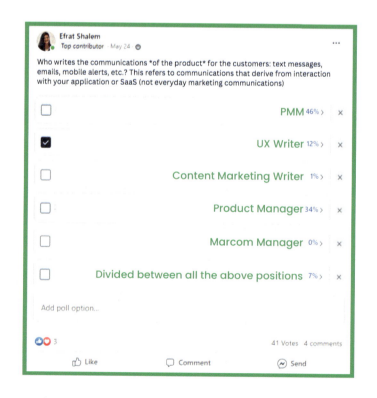

As you can see, my vote went to the UX Writer, and that is because UX writers are integrated into the product department and are ideally positioned to craft product communications. This stems from their unique skill set and perspective, combining a deep understanding of user experience with product knowledge.

Here are several reasons why UX writers are well-suited for this role:

1. User-centric focus: UX writers specialize in creating content that aligns with the user's journey and experience. They can ensure that product communications are user-centric and resonate with the audience.

2. Consistent tone and voice: UX writers are adept at maintaining a consistent tone and voice throughout the user interface. This consistency extends to product communication, providing a seamless and recognizable user experience.

3. Clarity and simplicity: Crafting concise and easily understandable messages is a core competency of UX writers. In the context of product communication, this is essential for conveying information effectively, especially in limited space, such as push notifications.

4. Collaboration with design: UX writers often collaborate closely with design teams, ensuring the content integrates seamlessly with the visual elements. This collaborative approach is valuable when creating both visually appealing and engaging product communications.

5. Behavior understanding: Understanding user behavior is a crucial aspect of UX writing. UX writers in the product department can leverage their user behavior insights to tailor product communications that resonate with the target audience.

To sum up, while product marketing managers and product managers play essential roles in shaping the overall product strategy and marketing messaging, UX writers bring a specialized skill set focused on enhancing the user experience through effective communication.

Therefore, incorporating UX writers into the process of crafting product communications contributes to a more holistic and user-centric approach. Thus, in the product communication ownership battle, the winner is the UX writer, who sits in the product department.

B2B & B2C TECH PRODUCT MARKETING

As outlined in this guide, product marketing managers function at the intersection of product development, marketing, growth, sales, and customer success. Their responsibility involves formulating and implementing targeted marketing strategies for specific products.

PMMs collaborate with various marketing departments, aligning with communications, content, design, and digital professionals. Beyond the marketing team, product marketing managers establish close partnerships with product and growth managers, UX designers, sales, customer success, and other stakeholders during a product launch.

A tech PMM is dedicating diverse efforts throughout the product lifecycle:

- **Pre-launch:** Interpret market, competitor, and customer research, influencing aspects like product features, user experience, naming, and packaging.

- **Launch:** Develop the product's go-to-market strategy, positioning, and messaging, and oversee mid and bottom-of-the-funnel content creation.

- **Post-launch:** Manage customer responses and surveys, help plan growth campaigns and experiments, and suggest improvements for future iterations.

The PMM position duties may vary based on the company's business model. B2B and B2C marketers speak the same language but with different dialects, and though their terms may align, their methods diverge due to distinct needs in both areas. Next, we will explore where B2B and B2C tech product marketing intersect and, more importantly, what sets them apart.

B2B AND B2C PMM SIMILARITIES

1. It is all human-to-human

Whether targeting the CEO of a million-dollar company or a freelancer pursuing their next gig, identifying the target audience is a foundational step in both domains. In both B2B and B2C product marketing, creating buyer personas or JTBDs is essential to comprehending audience characteristics, pain points, and needs. It is crucial to approach whoever is on the other end as a person.

2. Marketing and sales/customer success alignment

Collaboration between marketing and sales teams is crucial in both B2B and B2C. Defining buyer personas collectively and aligning on leads and conversions ensures an effective marketing-sales funnel. With that said, many product-led companies do not own a sales team at all, and they require a greater focus on customer success guidance and materials.

3. Data-driven ROI

Collecting, analyzing, and utilizing data from a company's initiatives is a common practice for revenue-focused strategies. Various businesses depend on diverse data sets, but both B2B and B2C product marketers focus on data-driven efforts to contribute to the company's bottom line. Without cold, hard facts, whether qualitative or quantitative, achieving growth becomes challenging regardless of the company's business model.

4. Go-to-market plans

While the journey to market for B2B and B2C products may vary, the planning process remains necessary and largely consistent. In both realms of product marketing, a highly effective go-to-market strategy is crucial for making the solution known to the audience.

B2B AND B2C PMM DIFFERENCES

1. Buyer types

B2C marketing focuses on individuals, considering factors like age, gender, and personal interests, whereas B2B marketing targets professionals, emphasizing job titles, company size, and budget, focusing on addressing buyer pain points.

2. Decision-makers

In B2C marketing, one decision-maker, the end consumer, drives the purchasing process. On the other hand, B2B sales cycles involve multiple decision-makers, such as product users, IT managers, finance, and other executives, requiring flexible marketing and sales-enablement materials.

3. Customer volume

B2B marketing targets a smaller client base compared to the larger consumer pool in B2C. As a result, B2B campaigns necessitate highly targeted approaches, while B2C allows more room for trial and error with a larger consumer base.

4. Sale cycle

B2C sales cycles are designed for speed, ease, and impulse purchases, often completed within 24 hours. In contrast, B2B sales cycles are inherently longer, involving thorough evaluations, budget considerations, and approvals from multiple decision-makers.

While B2B and B2C product marketing share commonalities, they are distinct entities with unique strategies, goals, tools, and execution timelines. Understanding the nuances is vital for product marketers to navigate and excel in both environments.

If you're a business leader looking to attract qualified product marketing manager candidates, keep the PMM job description clear with a brief list of duties, responsibilities, and qualifications. The list should be organized in bullet points, with each point accurately reflecting the job expectations. Stick to simple, direct language to tell candidates how they'll contribute to your organization's long-term success.

TECH PMM HIRING PROCESS & CAREER ADVANCEMENT

While the role of a product marketing manager may take various shapes and is not always clearly defined for hiring tech companies and candidates, it has gained tremendous popularity in recent years.

Therefore, throughout this guide, we tried to clarify the PMM position and delineated its responsibilities and how they manifest in both B2B and B2C tech companies while offering resolutions to common disputes.

Now, let's delve into the essential skills and qualifications that make a great tech PMM and what hiring managers should prioritize when evaluating candidates.

ESSENTIAL TECH PRODUCT MARKETER SKILLS

1. Customer empathy

PMMs need to immerse themselves in the customer perspective by maintaining curiosity and utilizing tools like interviews and surveys. Understanding the customer pain points and needs is vital to tailoring powerful messaging, GTM strategies, and products that fulfill their desires.

2. Data-driven approach

PMMs employ various user research tactics, such as surveys, product usage recordings, and heatmaps, to uncover valuable insights into the customer experience and behavior. A product marketer should be adept at extracting meaningful information from these research methods to generate effective marketing strategies and influence innovative product ideas and features throughout the product lifecycle.

3. Strategic thinking

PMMs perform best when they blend creativity with practicality to prioritize tasks and formulate impactful campaigns. Strategic thinking is essential for aligning marketing efforts with overarching business objectives and attaining return on investment.

4. Storytelling

PMMs should excel in the art of storytelling as it is a powerful tool to engage and connect with the audience emotionally. It transforms information into a narrative that is not only memorable but also resonates with the audience, making the product more relatable and appealing in a competitive market.

5. Organizational skills

PMMs must be extremely organized, given the demands of working on multiple projects simultaneously in a fast-paced, multifaceted environment. These organizational skills are essential for managing diverse tasks, timelines, and stakeholders. They ensure the marketing efforts align with broader business goals, timelines are met, and resources are optimized.

6. Cross-functional collaboration and communication

Collaborating with other teams is essential for PMMs, necessitating a thorough understanding of the broader business goals across various departments to enhance organizational effectiveness. Clear and constructive communication across all levels of the organization plays a pivotal role in internally conveying and sharing marketing messages and insights, ensuring that all stakeholders comprehend and are aligned with the overall vision, KPIs, and metrics.

7. Negotiation skills

These skills are crucial for PMMs dealing with internal stakeholders or external partners. PMMs navigate diverse opinions and priorities, making negotiation vital for achieving alignment. This includes negotiating budgets to execute the product marketing vision through large-scale, user-focused marketing initiatives.

8. Entrepreneurial mindset

PMMs surpass when they embody an entrepreneurial mindset with a proactive "get things done" approach. This attitude entails a willingness to take initiative, think creatively, and navigate ambiguity, aligning with the dynamic nature of marketing and product pioneering. It involves a proactive approach to problem-solving and a drive to explore and match innovative solutions to challenges.

9. Leadership abilities

PMMs should showcase exceptional leadership skills, encompassing not just steering the overall marketing strategy but also adeptly assigning responsibilities within a team. This leadership involves empowering team members to contribute their expertise and fostering a collaborative and high-performing environment. The ability to delegate tasks and responsibilities ensures that the team works cohesively toward common objectives. These skills will also enable ambitious PMMs to climb the corporate ladder to directors and VP of marketing roles.

Overall, these traits collectively contribute to the success of a tech product marketing manager in driving impactful and cohesive marketing strategies.

TRANSITIONING TO TECH PRODUCT MARKETING

- **English proficiency**

Fluency in English is essential for tech PMM positions, being the primary language of the industry. It facilitates effective communication with various stakeholders, encourages global collaboration, and ensures the successful dissemination of marketing strategies to international audiences.

- **Versatile marketing background**

Starting a career as a PMM in the tech sector typically demands a minimum of 2-3 years of marketing experience. Your professional journey can commence in various marketing fields, including content writing, marketing communications, or growth marketing.

Gaining diverse marketing experience enriches your comprehension of the buyer's journey across the marketing-sales funnel. It enhances your capacity to tailor holistic strategies to various marketing functions, resonating effectively with potential customers at different stages.

In addition, while a background in high tech is preferred, it is not mandatory. Exploring roles in companies offering technological solutions closely related to your industry background may provide a competitive advantage. For instance, serving as an eCommerce manager in a retail company could pave the way for transitioning to a PMM role at a marketplace tech company. As you refine your skills and accumulate valuable and diverse marketing experience, you better position yourself as a suitable and desirable candidate for a tech PMM role.

- **Education matters**

Though not a mandatory requirement for some tech companies, consider pursuing a bachelor's or master's degree, especially in marketing, to strengthen your foundational knowledge. An MBA can further enhance your skills, contributing to career advancement in the long run. Reading eBooks and blogs and taking focused professional courses is also a great way to gain practical inside knowledge from experts with extensive product marketing experience from leading tech companies.

- **Career advancement**

Working as a product marketer can progress to roles like senior or director PMM, eventually reaching VP of marketing positions. Alternatively, some individuals may transition to other marketing specializations or product-related roles, leveraging their diverse marketing backgrounds.

In summary, the journey to becoming a successful PMM involves starting from various marketing roles, gaining a comprehensive view of marketing, honing product marketing skills, and potentially advancing to leadership positions within the field.

PMM HIRING PROCESS IN HIGH-TECH

In my experience, an effective PMM hiring process is a well-defined, transparent, and structured series of steps:

1. Job description
A concise list of B2C/B2B/B2G responsibilities, duties, and qualifications, and a transparent salary range that varies according to experience and desirability.

2. Resume screening
Usually conducted by an HR representative, this stage involves a brief up to 45-minute phone or video call to discuss the candidate's resume, role responsibilities, and salary expectations to determine compatibility. Checking the candidate's website or portfolio and passing it to the hiring manager is crucial to evaluating their marketing skills, as there is no better showcase of a marketer's capabilities than how they promote themselves.

3. Direct manager video interview
The role of the direct manager is pivotal in the hiring process, as the decision to hire someone for their team hinges primarily on the chemistry with the candidate. Therefore, before requesting the candidate to invest extensive hours in home assignments, it is crucial that they first meet their potential direct manager. The purpose of this interview is to establish a working relationship and gain insights into job expectations and desired qualities. It is preferable that this meeting occurs over a video call rather than in-house. If the candidate successfully navigates the video interview and home assignment, the manager and team will meet them in person at a later stage, during a focused hiring day.

4. Home assignment
An effective home assignment is completed within a reasonable timeframe, ideally not exceeding 5 hours. It can focus on an imaginary product, a well-known product, a competing product, or a product of the candidate's choice. The goal is to provide an opportunity for the candidate to showcase their skills and talents without exploiting the situation for free work.

The assignment should be thoughtfully designed to align with the most relevant skills required for the PMM position, such as research, data analysis, storytelling, or strategic planning. To complement skills not showcased in the assignment, candidates can be asked to present another previous project they are proud of in the next stage of the hiring process, and given their field experience, they'd likely have ample projects to draw upon.

5. In-person presentation and team simulation
On a focused hiring day, the candidate meets the hiring manager and the team in person to showcase their work, understand the company culture, and answer and pose questions. All key members of the marketing and product teams should attend the presentation. This allows for the evaluation of the candidate's past achievements and preferred work style, and, most importantly, the assessment of team dynamics and communication.

6. HR final interview
The concluding HR interview serves to address any remaining queries, reaffirm salary expectations (without reductions from the initial agreement in the first HR interview, considering the candidate's investment in time and effort), and ensure the candidate's continued enthusiasm about joining the company. This interview can be conducted on-site after the team simulation or at a later date via a video call.

7. References
While I have reservations about this stage, as references can sometimes have unintended consequences, especially for exceptional candidates who may have surpassed their previous managers, it remains a common practice among tech companies. Yet, it's essential to prioritize the candidate's personality, attitude, talent, and skills over external opinions. Given the high competitiveness in the tech industry and the scarcity of great management, careful consideration is crucial in the hiring process.

This underscores the significance of tracking and onboarding empathetic and talented PMMs who can serve as exemplary leaders, fostering collaboration, excellence, and visualization of the marketing strategy for the entire company.

FINAL WORDS

TECH PRODUCT MARKETING SUMMARY

As we conclude our exploration of tech product marketing, let's revisit key insights that encapsulate the essence of this dynamic field:

1. Versatile marketing background

A diverse marketing background serves as the foundation for a thriving career in tech product marketing. It provides a comprehensive view of the marketing-sales funnel, empowering product marketers to craft creative and precise strategies for each marketing function and buyer journey stage.

2. Belongs to the marketing department

Product marketing is an integral part of the marketing department, playing a pivotal role in driving the success of products in the market.

3. First marketing function on board

Moreover, product marketing should take the lead as the first marketing function on board during the product development phase. This ensures a strategic, market-data-driven, and customer-centric approach from the initial stages, guiding the product's journey to launch.

4. Buyer journey improvement throughout the product life cycle

Product marketing's role goes beyond go-to-market (GTM) strategies. It emphasizes continuous improvement of the buyer journey throughout the entire product life cycle, adapting strategies as the product evolves.

5. Responsibilities vary by target market (B2C/B2B/B2B2C/B2G)

Whether it's business-to-consumer, business-to-business, or business-to-government, each market demands distinct messaging, channels, and tools, with the human-to-human approach serving as the guiding principle throughout.

6. Customer empathy

Product marketing serves as the customer's voice, comprehending and empathizing with the target audience to develop products and messages that resonate profoundly.

7. Entrepreneurial mindset

Product marketers should adopt a proactive and innovative problem-solving approach, leveraging market research, data, and decision-making techniques to formulate wise and effective marketing and product strategies that yield exceptional return on investment (ROI).

8. The leader and glue

Acting as the glue that connects product development with the marketplace, product marketing collaborates with stakeholders at all levels across almost every department, including product, sales, and customer success. It assumes a leadership role in shaping the general marketing strategy of the company.

9. Competitive field

Hiring companies and aspiring product marketing managers (PMMs) should acknowledge the competitiveness of the tech product marketing field. To thrive in this dynamic environment, continuous learning, adaptation, and strategic thinking are essential, and there should be deliberate efforts to attract empathetic, skilled, and wise marketing leaders who can shape the internal marketing vision and contribute significantly to its external realization, directly influencing the overall success of the company.

To sum up, as you kick off your adventure in tech product marketing, picture a thrilling ride filled with calculated strategies, a deep focus on customers, and the excitement of constant growth.

Your journey in tech product marketing is not just a job but a chance to be impactful and fulfilled. Embrace the twists and turns, celebrate your wins, and let your passion for improving every day drive you. You're always invited to return to this guide to refresh your memory.

Your path ahead is bursting with potential, and I believe your unique contributions can make waves in the tech industry and improve people's lives. Get ready for an exciting venture, and let your energy and ideas leave a lasting imprint.

Go, make your mark!

Made in the USA
Columbia, SC
09 July 2024